CHINA'S UNCERTAIN FUTURE

JEAN-LUC DOMENACH

TRANSLATED BY GEORGE HOLOCH

China's
UNCERTAIN FUTURE

COLUMBIA UNIVERSITY PRESS *New York*

Columbia University Press
Publishers Since 1893
New York   Chichester, West Sussex
cup.columbia.edu

Columbia University Press wishes to express its appreciation for assistance given by the government of France through the Ministère de la Culture in the preparation of this translation.

Ouvrange publié avec le concours du ministère français chargé de la culture — Centre national du livre.

Library of Congress Cataloging-in-Publication Data
Domenach, Jean-Luc.
    [Chine m'inquiète. English]
    The emergence of modern China / Jean-Luc Domenach ; translated by George Holoch.
        p. cm.
    Originally published in French under title : La Chine m'inquiète. Paris : Perrin, c2008.
    Includes bibliographical references and index.
    ISBN 978-0-231-15224-2 (cloth : alk. paper) — ISBN 978-0-231-52645-6 (e-book)
    1. China—Politics and government—2002–   2. China—Social conditions—2000–
3. China—Economic conditions—2000–   I. Title.
    DS779.4.D6613 2012
    951.06—dc23

                                                                    2012009452

Columbia University Press books are printed on permanent and durable acid-free paper.
This book is printed on paper with recycled content.

Printed in the United States of America
c 10 9 8 7 6 5 4 3 2 1

References to Internet Web sites (URLs) were accurate at the time of writing.
Neither the author nor Columbia University Press is responsible for URLs that may have expired or changed since the manuscript was prepared.

Contents

Acknowledgments

THIS BOOK IS A SEQUEL TO *COMPRENDRE LA CHINE D'AUJOURD'HUI*, published by Perrin in March 2007, and, like it, was inspired by a stay in Beijing from February 2002 to February 2007. This stay would not have been possible without the Ministry of Foreign Affairs and the French embassy in Beijing, whom I thank. But this book was written after my return to France and for that reason owes a good deal to the institution that again welcomed me, the Fondation Nationale des Sciences Politiques, and particularly to its Center for International Study and Research, which was warmly welcoming. I thank them as well.

Since my return, I have been welcomed by another "unit" (*danwei* in Chinese), the Perrin publishing house, where I direct the Asies series. I wish to express to all those involved the pleasure I experience in our collaboration and particularly to thank Anthony Rowley for his friendly lucidity and Marie-Laure Defretin for her warm professionalism.

My gratitude also goes to Thierry Pech, who gave me some luminous advice, as well as to Geneviève Domenach-Chich and Diana Hochraich, who read a first version of this book.

Introduction

The New "Chinese Moment"

CHINA IS NOW JUST AROUND THE CORNER. ONE-FOURTH OF THE bars-tabacs in Paris are Chinese owned, and you cannot take the Métro without seeing students or businessmen from Beijing. In September 2007, a Chinese warship for the first time dropped anchor in a French port on the Mediterranean, a stone's throw from fashionable beaches.[1]

This is a worldwide phenomenon. The paths of Chinese emigration traverse Russia and central Europe. The leader of the parliamentary opposition in Australia has touted his knowledge of Mandarin as part of his 2007 election campaign strategy.[2] Chinese companies are doing business throughout Africa, much to the chagrin of Westerners, who thought they owned the territory.

This sudden spread of the Chinese presence is the effect of an economic triumph that has made history: an average annual growth rate of 9 percent for three decades, driven by foreign trade—the third largest in the world—and particularly by exports. As a result, although socially poor, China is rich in its currency reserves. Except for top-of-the-line technology and cultural products, nothing escapes from its commercial empire: it controls 70 percent of the world market of Paris mushrooms, and the statuettes of saints bought in Brazil are made in China.[3]

China is not only more visible; it is more important. Western leaders no longer travel to Beijing to make sure the dragon is still sleeping or to question it about its region. They come to speak to it about world affairs, to ask that it reduce its exports, and to secure contracts to support their own economies. It is not an accident that President Sarkozy's diplomatic adviser, Jean-David Levitte, was a trained specialist in Chinese and Asian affairs.

All these developments point to the rapid rise of China toward the top of the world hierarchy. And the least that one can say is that this event has not provoked ordinary reactions. Whereas the rise of Japan forty years ago was generally ignored, the progress of China has produced discordant responses around the world. That progress is sometimes admired and often exaggerated. Jacques Chirac, for instance, declared off the bat in a speech at Beijing University on October 26, 2006, that he considered China a serious candidate for the leadership of world affairs. Sometimes—particularly among journalists and human rights advocates—people exaggerate or extrapolate. And they denounce the machinery set up by the Chinese leadership to deceive the world and exploit their own people—for "China provides the spectacle of a marriage of neoliberalism with communism."[4]

All in all, there are very few who, like Lucien Bianco, have kept a cool head and think that "the accession to the status of world power of a nation-continent containing one-fifth of humanity merely corrects an anomaly."[5] The European public views China primarily as a threat: people wonder what would be left of the West if the Chinese succeeded in investing as much intelligence in their economy as they have in labor. And what will happen to world oil reserves when per capita Chinese energy consumption reaches the level of the most developed countries?[6] Reactions vary depending on the degree of confidence people have in their own country. Only the English have a majority of optimists (60 percent). The anxious amount to 57 percent of Germans, 60 percent of Italians, and 64 percent of the French.[7] So what does the future hold? Susan Shirk, a former White House adviser on the Far East, is worried: with respect to present-day China, she speaks of "the rule that rising powers cause war."[8]

It is as though, after the idealization of the Cultural Revolution and the denunciation of the June 1989 massacre, a new "China moment" was taking shape in public opinion, one characterized by a kind of stupefaction in which admiration is mixed with fear, as though we were nothing but prey at the mercy of the dragon of the Far East, as though the long history that led the West to dominate the world had been reduced to nothing, as though its inner strength had disappeared in a few decades.

I have striven to remain impervious to fashionable currents, such as the French "Maoists" of the past and, more recently, the ill-informed observers who refuse to take into account the changes brought about by economic growth. I have formed, or rather reformed, my judgment over the course of my years spent in Beijing, from February 2002 to February 2007. To my great surprise, I have come to realize that many Chinese have a much more realistic assessment than one might imagine—sometimes a frankly pessimistic one—of the huge gap that still separates them from the West. Many think that present-day China is large without being great and that it is not a modern country but a vast and unevenly developed work in progress. The impression of power it gives off derives from its huge population and the immense space it occupies, but its modern sector is confined to a few metropolises.[9]

I asked myself what motivated the pessimism of my interlocutors, and I investigated. Relying on books recently published in China, I considered its history of violence and failure, which the Chinese economic triumph of the last three decades has not succeeded in making people forget about. In addition, my immersion in China led me to see that the existing polemical positions on the country are contradicted by the facts. For example, it is thought that because it has not developed democracy, China has not been struck by economic incompetence and political paralysis. In fact, although it has developed a victorious economic strategy, it has not overcome the many serious dangers that still affect its growth. Finally, if the communist regime were as effectively authoritarian as both its advocates and its enemies believe, its leaders would have already forced the application of the rather reasonable economic policy that they have recently adopted.

I came to understand that the Chinese man in the street is deeply right to evaluate dispassionately the outcome of the thirty "glorious" years of Deng Xiaoping's policies: after all, after so much suffering, this was the least that the communist government had to do to hope to secure the forgiveness of History. And I internalized his caution, because the problem is not the present but the future. When the cymbals of triumph finally fall silent, China will be confronted with a moment of truth. Only then will we know whether it can become a great modern country.

CHINA'S UNCERTAIN FUTURE

Book I

Measure for Measure

WHAT IS THE STATE OF CHINA? OBSERVERS GENERALLY SEEM TO agree that in the last three decades China has made enormous economic progress, significant gains in foreign policy, and relative advances in social and cultural matters, but little political progress—and even less when it comes to human rights. But they have divergent views of the importance of these various sectors. Some analysts believe that economic progress will bring about improvements in everything else; others, that the lack of democracy will in the end produce catastrophe. It is not surprising that the former are generally close to business circles and are well connected in Beijing. The latter are often intellectuals who believe that the defeat of the dissident movement has done nothing to invalidate the maxim of its founder, Wei Jinsheng: "Without the introduction of a democratic system, China will be unable to develop in a stable and durable way."[1]

The position I set forth here strives to take into account the arguments of both sides but contends that they often exaggerate: either they do not relate statistics to the size of the Chinese territory and the country's population and do not pay sufficient attention to the huge cost of the economic progress that has been realized, or they do not grant sufficient importance to the huge effects of economic progress and pay no attention to the problems that rapid democratization would have posed and would still pose. This position is based on a judgment made by Lucien Bianco: "The development of China over the last quarter century is as different from the Maoist period as the Empire was from the French Revolution."[2] Hence, it is as pointless to exaggerate as it is to deny the elements of continuity.

Chapter 1

The Regime's New Foundations

The End of Totalitarianism

CONTRARY TO WELL-ESTABLISHED STEREOTYPES, THE CHINESE political regime was both renewed and consolidated. The essential event was the end not of communism but of totalitarian communism: the country is still governed dictatorially by the Chinese Communist Party, but this dictatorship has assumed less power over people and events than the former Maoist regime.

The way in which Deng saved a regime that Maoist frenzy had plunged into misfortune, disorder, and impotence is now well known. Upon returning to power in December 1978, he promised to concentrate his efforts on concrete growth, and he took preliminary measures to boost incomes. To consolidate the trust that his prestige had earned him, he immediately abolished the least bearable aspects of Maoist totalitarianism and released a number of political prisoners. Then in the 1980s, while reaffirming the political monopoly of the CCP, he institutionalized the regime, decentralized the economy, dismantled the people's communes, and authorized the emergence of a nonstate sector.[1] This gradual transition appeared to be threatened by the tragic events of Tiananmen Square in 1989. But instead of allowing himself to be trapped politically by the bloody repression he had ordered, Deng was able to take advantage of it to accelerate economic reform and the opening of the nation to the world without causing anyone in the CCP to fear that "class enemies" would benefit.

Deng granted priority to economic development, with the goal of saving the communist regime and ensuring its long-term survival. But if the population were to go back to work, it could no longer be stifled. The shift from totalitarianism to what the American scholar Minxin Pei calls "developmental autocracy" meant a transition from mass terror to increasingly selective repression and more flexible control.[2] The results after three decades are considerable.

Today, prisons and labor camps hold only a small number of political prisoners—probably a few thousand or a few tens of thousands, if one includes prisoners from various sects, such as the Falun Gong: too many, of course, but China is no longer one of the world leaders in repression. The Chinese gulag has not been dismantled, and the carceral situation varies, depending on location, from very bad, through bad, to almost correct, but arbitrariness is in retreat, and the range of application of official legislation is growing. Generally, we have witnessed an explosion in the use of law: the number of trials almost tripled between 1987 and 2003, and the number of judges increased from seventy thousand to 180,000 between 1988 and 2004.[3] Courts and prosecutors have been seeking to assert themselves against the security forces, and not all trials are fixed in advance, particularly because lawyers have been promised a law guaranteeing legal immunity for their statements in court. Trials have become more effective in dealing with labor disputes.[4] Similarly, citizens' complaints against the state—hence against local administrations—will soon be treated more impartially, because they will be judged by tribunals at a distance from local courts.[5] The death penalty, which is unfortunately very popular in public opinion, is practiced on a scale unknown in any other country in the world, although the rate has declined since the requirement that each decision must be confirmed by the Supreme Court was enacted. One positive sign is the fact that the Chinese authorities noted as a success the decline in the number of executions in 2006. According to Amnesty International, the number was still between 7,500 and 8,500—enormous, but the tendency is clearly downward.[6] Though theoretically prohibited, torture has not disappeared, but it is more and more frequently punished, as is the abominable traffic in the organs of executed prisoners, which is one of the disgraces of contemporary China.[7]

The fundamental change is that the Chinese Communist Party has abandoned any ambition to bring about a global transformation. Mass campaigns have become less frequent and weaker, control over the population has relaxed, and the surveillance of private life in urban settings has been abolished. For example, on October 1, 2003, to the almost total indifference of the foreign press, an essential element of totalitarianism was eliminated in Beijing (after it had been in most other cities): the requirement that anyone getting married present a certificate of good conduct drawn up by their party unit, which had guaranteed the power of party committees over private life; in reality, changes in housing and economic organization had increasingly reduced its application. Soon thereafter, all city dwellers received the right to a passport with no prior certificate from the police or their employer.[8] These two measures symbolized the definitive end of the totalitarian system.

But this positive development has not prevented a massive increase in the violation of social rights, stemming from the new importance of the economy and hence of money to the communist leadership.

The difficult situation of Chinese women is largely attributable to the fact that they are subject to commerce of every variety. This situation is little known outside the country because it is not very visible and often denied in China, even by the women themselves involved.[9] China is one of the few countries in which more women than men commit suicide. The proportion of women in responsible positions of any kind is the smallest, and female workers are subject to the most brutal domination.[10]

This situation is preserved by habits developed before communism, by the "innovations" of the Maoist period (which liberated women only as workers), and by the recent commercialization of the female sex. But it is certain that the public authorities, especially in villages, bear very heavy responsibility in these matters.

Moreover, it is as workers that Chinese citizens are most ill treated today. Despite the press campaign organized by the authorities in the summer of 2007 and the publication of penalties imposed on companies, very few of them respected the official legislation. Four companies out of five did not sign employment contracts with their workers before a law applicable in January 2008 was adopted, and companies are already working to sidestep it; at least they are now denounced by the press and sometimes sanctioned by courts.[11] Failure to respect the law helps explain the incredible number of workplace accidents—there were 127,000 deaths in 2005—[12] and the level of worker discontent prevalent in several industrial sectors, particularly in mining: in many places, particularly in Shanxi, local officials make private investments in illegal coal mines where accidents are frequent and deadly. But workers rarely dare to organize because they are overseen by thugs hired by the bosses. Indeed, companies themselves often assume police powers: an American correspondent reported that he had been detained by factory thugs and that the police on the scene dared not intervene.[13] Migrant workers are subject to authoritarian treatment, even to forms of slavery, as several scandals in 2007 demonstrated. In all these cases, companies benefit from the complicity of local authorities.

A Chinese Recipe: Relaxed Authoritarianism

There still remain some traits from the Maoist period. For example, the rulers reside in the same imperial park that Mao Zedong and his companions occupied in 1949, a stone's throw from the Forbidden City. Very few visitors are admitted, and the highest-ranking authorities almost never grant interviews. Yet the regime has reduced its political objectives—it promises that China will remain for more than fifty years in the "primary phase of socialism." The principle of the nationalization of the land has lost substance in cities, where one can theoretically secure ownership rights lasting seventy years. Moreover, the authorities have decollectivized all agricultural production and denationalized one half of the production in other sectors, while of course preserving its domination over essential sectors and indirect control over the economy as a whole.

Political control of society has not disappeared, but it has been relaxed. Opposition activities are still repressed, but individual opinions circulate freely within families and, with some precaution, in the circle of one's friends and colleagues. Things are different for the publication of nonconformist opinions. Control of cinema, publishing, and the news media is constant and sophisticated, although much less strict than in the past. Every film proposal must be submitted to the authorities in advance, and only twenty foreign films a year are authorized to be shown. But overall, censorship is less harsh. The publishing industry is much more diverse and open to foreign literature. In 2005, more than two hundred thousand new titles were published, an overall increase of 6.8 percent—including a 20 percent increase in the social and human sciences.[14] More and more books are contributing to preserving the memory of ancient China and of the heroic founders of the regime—but also the memory of recent suffering, particularly family tragedies.[15]

Similarly, the regime has maintained solid control over news media, focusing on a few strategic sectors: headlines, editorials, and television news are all the same. This control is so powerful and ubiquitous that it usually requires no repressive measures. The jailing of journalists, denounced by human rights groups, involving about thirty thousand of the 550,000 Chinese journalists, is usually the result of reprisals ordered by local mafias and not the central government. The press has in fact criticized provincial authorities with increasing frequency: for example, the authorities in Fujian exploded in anger against the New China News Agency for what they considered its negative reporting on the way they had dealt with serious flooding.

Press control operates in every organ through hierarchical circuits that leave room for personal rivalries, professional disagreements, and editorial differences. Therefore, although news reporting is generally biased, the bias is uneven, and this allows fragments of the truth to slip through, enabling readers or listeners to form their own judgment. I am acquainted with a taxi driver, for example, who has over the years developed real expertise on crises in the Middle East by listening to bulletins on the official radio: "I stick to the facts that they broadcast, and then I think for myself and manage to discover the facts that were omitted at first," he told me.

The central government has, with increasing frequency, even found it advantageous to reveal local scandals. For example, in January 2000, a Sichuan daily revealed the scandal of contaminated blood in Henan and, in the summer of 2007, journalists exposed a case of industrial slavery.[16] But the freedom conceded in this way is limited and transitory. Only a few publications, such as *Southern Weekend*, have managed to specialize in investigative journalism, but the scope of its autonomy is constantly under threat.

New media are much harder to control. Recently in Davos, the CEO of China Mobile ingenuously revealed that he gave the authorities all the information about his customers that they requested. It is also well known that in many places official propaganda can automatically be spread through mobile phones. But it does seem hard to monitor the text messaging and conversations of six hundred million users, and experience demonstrates that many popular protests have been organized by means of conversations in code on mobile phones.[17]

The same thing is true for the Internet, which has about four hundred million users in China. Of course, the authorities have created remarkable technical teams in the State Council Information Office that were able, in October 2007, to block for several hours the American search engines Google, Yahoo, and Live and automatically redirect users to the Chinese site Baidu.[18] But users are adept at adopting clever and constantly changing maneuvers, which leads to increasingly brutal campaigns of government repression: the closing of cyber cafés, the destruction of some sites or electronic addresses, and police raids.[19] But international protests against repeated attempts by the Chinese authorities to assert their control and intimidate foreign sites should not be allowed to conceal the fact that the Web in China has become an extraordinary window on the world and a real platform for expressing opinions.

It is on this shifting and multifarious stage that the great changes in the future are probably taking shape. According to a recent survey, 53 percent of Chinese Web users think they express themselves more freely on the Web than in real life, and 50 percent acknowledge that their use of the Internet has changed their personality.[20] The authorities know it and are worried about these subterranean changes to the people's state of mind. This was probably part of what Hu Jintao was alluding to when he complained in his report to the Seventeenth Congress of the CCP in October 2007 that "our achievements . . . sometimes fall short of the expectations of the people . . . people today are more independent, more selective, and more changeable."[21]

As elsewhere, then, the Internet in China is a space for information and socialization as well as for the circulation of opinions. It is the site of spontaneous mobilizations, either around the social concerns of the moment (for example, the cost of housing in the summer of 2007) or very often around nationalist themes (for example, when Renault used a photograph of Mao in one of its ads). E-mail has also made possible the establishment of lists of interlocutors, and these are the embryos of associations; I myself have been a member of several of them. Their sponsors are, of course, under surveillance but have not been seriously bothered so far. Blogs are proliferating, and most of their authors have succeeded in remaining anonymous. Overall, a great deal of information circulates through these channels. In the face of these massive phenomena, the arrest of fifty cyberdissidents is scandalous but secondary.[22]

The Birth of a Public Opinion?

Consider the first mobilization carried out by the Internet. In the spring of 2003, during the SARS episode, the anger of Web users spread out into the urban population at large and forced the authorities to take action against the epidemic; on that occasion, e-mails and SMS messages won out over the incompetence of the Beijing municipal government.[23]

This episode revealed not only major weaknesses in the control of information but also a shift in public opinion. This was mostly limited to major urban centers, and it was not entirely novel: during the totalitarian period, analogous movements had arisen in response to the regime's hesitations, some explicit, others more diffuse. But it seems that a new cycle began with the massive layoffs in industry that the Chinese government carried out in the mid-1990s, which provoked protest demonstrations and widespread expressions of solidarity. Moreover, nationalist sentiment provoked disturbances on several occasions in large cities, notably in May 1999 against the American bombing of the Chinese embassy in Belgrade and against Japan in 2005. Other subjects of general interest also provoked movements in public opinion: natural disasters, epidemics, scandals in the health system, workplace accidents, public transportation, evictions caused by "urban renewal," and, increasingly, environmental problems.

These movements can lead to public demonstrations. In large cities, the installation of a polluting factory may encounter an angry population and even opposition from city officials. In Xiamen, in Fujian province, popular protest has until now blocked the proposed installation of a chemical factory, and in Shanghai white-collar workers were still fighting in early 2008 against an extension of the "supertrain" from the airport into the urban area that risked ruining their environment and diminishing their property values.[24] In other places, an increase in transportation costs might provoke a riot.

These mobilizations sometimes produce their effects in the open. Opinion surveys, increasingly popular in the press, express the growing boldness of public opinion. For example, *China Youth Daily* reported in the summer of 2006 that more than 70 percent of Chinese would be opposed to an inheritance tax. And around the same time, the *Beijing Youth Daily* blandly noted that "more than 80 percent of the Chinese are worried about the safety of medicines in the marketplace."[25]

If public opinion has grown bolder, this is also because the attitude of the authorities has begun to change, something too often neglected by foreign observers. Some leaders have expressed their respect for ordinary people, and Prime Minister Wen Jiabao does not hesitate to display his compassion to the victims of climate disasters or health accidents. During the major New Year storms in 2008, the nine topmost Chinese leaders went to express their compassion to travelers blocked in railroad stations and to other victims. Official propaganda praises leaders, who do not hesitate to rally public opinion. In cases of natural disaster, local authorities are now judged by both their public opinion and the central government. The government has ordered that secrecy about the number of victims be ended and has forbidden—in principle—local governments to prevent the discontented to go to Beijing to complain.[26] Any scandal now provides the government with the opportunity to deal ruthlessly with those responsible and to remind their colleagues that it is in their interest to keep "harmonious" the society they have in their charge.

Of course, the lower levels of the political-administrative apparatus demonstrate all kinds of resistance to this new course. The regime being what it is, local authorities have hardly developed the habit of consulting their constituents. Indeed, depending on power relations and local conditions, the expression of public opinion is encouraged (and directed to the extent possible), simply accepted, manipulated, or crushed.

In the Country of Microclimates

This extreme diversity of conditions reveals an important characteristic of the political situation over the last three decades. Whereas the means of communication were constantly improving and the "work units" established by Maoist communism were collapsing in the cities, the cellular structure of the administration grew stronger in the vast Chinese territory. Much more than in the past, China is made up of a multitude of cells subject to the law of their chieftains—the American authority on China Michel Oksenberg went so far as to speak of "fragmented authoritarianism" to characterize the Chinese political regime.[27]

This fragmentation is first and foremost the effect of a geography that contains enormous diversity within regional subdivisions.[28] It was revived by granting autonomy to the cells of the former totalitarian control system.[29] It also depends on an economic policy—the policy of Deng Xiaoping—that based the modernizing surge on decentralization and competition between localities and then shifted responsibility for public services and their financing to local communities, an excellent pretext for predation by officials.[30] Guy Sorman reports: "According to Chinese government estimates, 40 percent of taxes taken from the peasants have no legal basis and never go into the public coffers."[31]

In this way, what Minxin Pei calls "local predatory states" have been established.[32] Local interests presented as the most legitimate take precedence over the rules of law and morality, and all sorts of lunacy becomes possible. In the district of Fumin, in Yunnan, for example, leaders decided to complete their ecological work by covering the mountain facing their offices with green paint.[33] The least pessimistic scholars acknowledge that in areas that are not priorities for Beijing, particularly in the countryside, local officials are relatively free: they take advantage of their freedom without hesitation to seize a variable portion of peasant taxes and to engage in land transactions in the name of the state.[34]

This phenomenon is not new—in the 1950s a district official in Henan supported a theater company[35]—but it was accelerated by political détente and economic decentralization. By the 1990s, it was possible to note in various provinces, including Shanxi, the rise of feelings of local identity.[36] On essential problems today the regime seems to be divided not horizontally, between various factions in the central leadership, but vertically, between the dominant faction in the center and a very complex provincial and local apparatus that does not always apply official economic policy.[37]

Within this apparatus, provincial leaders theoretically have great influence, but lower-level officials can wield literally feudal powers. All of them in general enjoy exorbitant advantages, some material and some tied to the exercise of power and their connections. From the city level upward, they have good living conditions, often with new offices and official housing, and feast at will. A significant minority strives to work honestly or makes moral rigor an element in their career: I have met some of them. But it seems that most do not hesitate to use their influence to help their families and to collect bribes or, even better, free shares of stock.

They often enjoy close protection from the police, who have their own interests, for example in prostitution—the position as director of security of a city is much sought after. Families of leaders sometimes regulate their affairs personally, with no fear of the consequences; for example, the relatives of a leader in Luoyang who had just died in a hospital went so far as to beat four nurses whom they considered responsible.[38]

However, the cellular structure of the territory can also foster the more positive phenomena of the politicization of rural communities, as shown by the village elections that involved more than 110 million peasants in early 2004.[39] Many observers have scornfully pointed out that they were not perfectly democratic—which is plausible—but it does appear that the elections were not completely rigged. If the authorities authorized these elections, this was in part to limit property seizures and illegitimate violence as well as to renew local CCP officials who often served clans rather than the party, and this is what seemed to occur in many cases: the elections fostered the application of official policy but also provided more genuine attention to the population. But only the future will tell whether the extension of village elections since 1997 will make possible the Chinese equivalent of the training of republican elites in nineteenth-century rural France that Maurice Agulhon has so brilliantly analyzed.[40]

Chinese NGOs illustrate a second positive effect of territorial fragmentation. Most of them are engaged in purely local activity, such as help for the aged and community services.[41] They often enjoy some degree of freedom because their work is local and they have the support of village and district officials. Their number is usually underestimated, because observers disregard the fact that many of them are not officially registered—three hundred thousand are recognized, but more than two million are in existence.[42] And their influence is denigrated on the pretext that they manifest at least formal loyalty to the regime; besides, a 1998 circular from the Organization Department of the CCP encouraged the establishment of party cells in NGOs.[43]

But this is to forget that under current conditions in China—the crushing of democratic dissidence and the economic and diplomatic triumph of the communist government—no influence is possible except within the regime. For example, one NGO very active in the defense of migrant women benefits from its close connections to the official Women's Federation and from the personal relations of its president, who is the daughter of a major writer whom Zhou Enlai appreciated, a delegate to the Chinese People's Consultative Conference, and a frequent guest at the Davos Forum. But the effectiveness of an NGO in the field depends primarily on its relations with local authorities, who determine the scope of its role as a source of information and politicization. This seems to be particularly true of NGOs devoted to protecting the environment, which, according to recent studies, have been able to play a real role in social mobilization.[44]

The Chinese territory is an area of microclimates, some marked primarily by the criminalization of government, others by open debate of major local problems, and most probably combining the two.

The Serfs Have Become Individuals

There nonetheless remains a general area over which the central government has the power to act. But the nature of those acts has changed. Under Mao Zedong, they consisted of violent mobilization entirely directed toward the future. At present, the government no longer merely promises benefits and crushes dissent. It also carries out or makes possible positive developments that are both concrete and verifiable and that anyone can measure in terms of money and purchasing power: a richer diet, better housing, leisure activities.

The central government no doubt adopted this policy for anything but philanthropic reasons. Its original purpose was to protect and consolidate the communist regime, and in that it succeeded. But once the principal emphasis shifted from the political to the economic field, the people increased in importance. They stopped being a shapeless mass of individuals who could be mobilized and exploited at will and became a necessary, and therefore respectable, set of producers and consumers whose individuality had to be recognized. It was necessary not only to control this necessary individual but also to respect and speak to him.

It was inevitable that this new autonomy would also reach into the realm of private life. It has happened over the last few decades in cities and more slowly in the countryside. The importance attributed to private life has increased. In the past supervised and bestowed, it has become free, and personal choices have grown in diversity. Today, one can find homosexual nightclubs, and on Sunday mornings, devotees of the most bizarre leisure activities meet on the outskirts of cities. The improbable has gradually come to pass: individuals—primarily in cities, it's true—have started to defend their private freedom. A young married couple sentenced to a prison term for having watched a pornographic movie successfully appealed their sentence. More recently, two young residents of Shanghai taped kissing in the subway sued the Shanghai Metro Company because the video showed up on the Web.[45] These changes are laying the groundwork for the future, because everyone knows, and many are already saying, that it will not forever be possible to deny public freedom to individuals to whom private freedoms have already been granted.

The recognition of a form of individuality has already produced a kind of economic partnership between the government and the population. As the rightness of the wager on growth was verified, the governing circles evolved from the idea of prosperity granted to the more or less conscious practice of contractual prosperity, whereby the serfs of the past have become both individual producers and individual consumers who are indispensable for growth. And the leaders have called on the people to consume more and have promised increased pay.

This is a new and formidable situation. For the first time, the Chinese people have been granted not yet the political right to express their opinion but the practical right to participate autonomously in the process of producing and consuming essential for the future of all. Although the Chinese people have no greater access to democracy than before, their economic collaboration is publicly considered indispensable, which has conferred on them an entirely different status from that of the past, guaranteeing them not merely survival but a minimum of attention and respect on the part of their masters.

Individuals have taken advantage of this status to increase their earnings, although they have not turned to independent unions or politics, which have the twofold disadvantage of being forbidden and dangerous. In an expanding economy that needs skilled manpower, the most effective way of progressing is to establish competition between companies. After proving himself for a few months, an employee asks for a raise and, if it is not granted, he quits to go work for the company across the way. This is why so many Chinese hotels have been built near their rivals in the major international chains—they are certain they can hire away, for a few extra pennies, the personnel trained in Western methods. All available sources confirm the remarkable mobility of the Chinese work force: every year, about 33 percent of managers in the service sector quit their jobs.[46] Western employers see the perfect secretary they have meticulously trained and who they believed was devoted to their service for the long term disappear in the blink of an eye.

Everyone has his or her own reality in today's China. Among the people at the top, there is plunder and the accumulation of family fortunes. And for the people of the "hundred surnames" (the common people), there is the race for higher wages and bargain prices. Who said Chinese workers worked for the sake of work, from some kind of ethical imperative, rather than for money? Whoever did should look closer at how the workforce circulates between major factory areas, mobile phones held to their ears, and how employees can discreetly nap when supervision relaxes. City dwellers are told to consume? Well, they consume the way their forebears were said to have made the revolution: by means of constant guerilla warfare. One has to see how people adopt multiple tactics to acquire a product at the best price. The collective behavior of travelers has also changed. In the past, airline delays were considered an inevitable element in the bureaucratic order of the world. Today, once the first hour of passivity has gone by, the temperature rises, protests explode, and violence looms.

The very society that was impressive because of its discipline thirty years ago has now become a much more agitated society, one in which everyone works, consumes, and lives for himself. It is a society of labor, but one that is increasingly moved by the working population itself, in which a vast movement of social emancipation is taking shape, governed by the established partnership with the government. This movement is seldom interpreted as a whole. Observers take note of the fierce Chinese desire for money and leisure but illustrate it with amusing or even ridiculous anecdotes, ones typical of a supposedly naïve practice of capitalism. But where is the naïveté? Chinese workers and consumers fully understand how the system in which they are living operates. They fully understand its harshness and have adapted to it, but they never miss an opportunity to enjoy its advantages. I might add another anecdote, a moving and significant one. In the bedding section of an Ikea store in Beijing, dozens of customers fall asleep on the mattresses, worn out by their week's work and happy to experience modern comfort.

The caricature of the alleged Chinese taste for capitalism is generally matched by the opposite cliché: solemn attention is called to the indeed increasing number of social disturbances—seventy-five thousand in 2005—breaking out around the country. And it is claimed that they threaten the regime. Some commentators do not hesitate to state that Chinese leaders "fear for their power." Really! Has Hu Jintao confided any secrets? Has the guard around Zhongnanhai, the cabinet offices, and provincial governments been reinforced? Obviously not. The government does not feel threatened because it is not threatened.

It is true that the wealth and the brutality of local officials has provoked the majority of these incidents. But the recently gained awareness, which everyone has, of his new right to receive his due has made injustice and theft unacceptable: this moral claim expresses the whole difference from the past. Disturbances that have a political dimension at the outset are infrequent. Most of them are what might be called conflicts of distribution: a territorially limited population rises up because it believes itself to have been unjustly expropriated, or inadequately compensated for land confiscated from it, or because it has suffered harm (for example, the suspension of pension payments).

In the face of these abuses, the protesters often formulate offers of negotiation in a vocabulary that is both moderate and conventional. But they seldom bear fruit, because the powerful are not exactly in the habit of compromising. Besides, local officials are operating inside a hierarchy that generally dissuades them from giving in and provides them with police help.[47] They therefore often respond with attempts at intimidation that provoke from the other side a swift resort to violence.

The history of China includes countless examples of rebellion. Under Mao Zedong, they generally came in response to irremediably tragic situations, as during the terrible famine of the Great Leap Forward. Now, in contrast, they are more widespread and frequent, not only because repression has diminished but because they are motivated by moral reasons.[48] These reasons make it possible to organize vigorous and combative solidarity, but such solidarity remains localized. For example, the expansion of the Beijing airport was seriously slowed, as was the construction of the Narita airport near Tokyo more than thirty years ago, by the resistance of a village, like that of Astérix, that regularly routed the forces of order. All of Beijing observed, with simultaneous amusement and jealousy, the resistance of the invincible village, but no one risked attributing any political importance to it.

A New Class Struggle?

Then why do so many observers give so much emphasis to social conflict in present-day China? Because most of them are influenced by the model of the class struggle that accompanied the industrial revolution in nineteenth-century Europe: no capitalist triumph without a social catastrophe. And some find it provocative to apply this model to a political regime that still calls itself communist.

This interpretation is supported by a powerful argument. Chinese society is one of the most inegalitarian in the world: its Gini coefficient is 0.46, which is on par with Zimbabwe and worse than the United States. The most pronounced inequality is that dividing city from countryside. An old disparity perpetuated under Mao Zedong, it had begun to be reduced in the early 1980s, but it later increased, reaching an income difference of 3.2 to 1 in 2003. In the province of Jilin between 1983 and 2005, the annual income of city dwellers quintupled, while that of the peasants merely doubled.[49] This economic inequality is intensified by social and cultural disparity, because the world of the countryside is distant from everything that counts.

The second inequality is the one dividing the very rich, 90 percent of whom are said to be sons of party officials, from all the others. The 20 percent most disadvantaged in the population, for instance, receive only 2.75 percent of national income. On the other hand, China has sixty-six billionaires and 440,000 millionaires (in euros), which places it fifth in the world, in front of France and Italy, whereas three hundred million of its inhabitants live on less than one dollar a day.[50] And 45 percent of the national wealth (50 percent in Jilin) is held by the richest 10 percent of the population (primarily concentrated in Guangzhou, Shanghai, and Beijing and the provinces of Jiangsu, Shandong, and Liaoning). Sixty million people have annual incomes above twenty thousand dollars.[51] They are the members of the privileged class that sprang from the political and administrative apparatus.

It is harder to identify other social classes. One can see the outlines of a city-dwelling mass often sharing the same housing conditions in large developments and confronting the same problems, particularly pollution and transportation difficulties. But there are huge disparities between its various components, making it hard to identify the famous "middle stratum" courted by Western perfumers and jewelers, apart from its habit of frequenting stores like Carrefour and Ikea. Often, it amounts to the same thing as the privileged class just mentioned. Information available about this middle class, in which so many forecasters have invested their hope, is weak and vague. For Gilles Guiheux, it amounts to between 10 and 20 percent of the population. We are awaiting with interest the confirmation of hypotheses formulated by Jean-Louis Rocca, according to which the lifestyle of this nebulous middle class indicates a combination of individual modernity and moral and political neoconservatism.[52]

For its part, the "proletariat" is subject to contradictory currents. The working-class aristocracy formed by communism has been partially destroyed, which has engendered revolts by the unemployed, whose language and mode of action sometimes recalls Western movements. A new proletariat from the countryside has appeared; its living conditions are very harsh and its ranks bloated: there are more than 150 million migrant workers. But the least that can be said is that the catastrophic forecasts it inspired have not been confirmed: this subproletariat has not revolted, particularly because everything seems preferable to the life it has left behind. Moreover, the central government has been promising since 2003–2004 to improve conditions for migrants. The improvement has been real but slow and seems primarily the result of a gradual rise in wages.

The peasants, finally, whose universal condition was recently close to serfdom, experienced very varied outcomes after their liberation from the people's communes—there is not much in common between the rich peasants of Jiangsu, the impoverished peasants of the wheat fields of Henan, and those who are hanging on to existence in the arid steppes of the northwest. The peasant world is subject to powerful migratory movements that empty the poorest (often rugged) parts of the most heavily populated provinces. The authorities are aware of the problem. In January 2004, "Document No. 1" of the Central Committee of the CCP was for the first time devoted to Chinese peasants, and many concrete measures were subsequently adopted, although localities usually failed to apply them. Collection of the agricultural tax was supposedly halted in January 2006, but evidence gathered leads to the suspicion that it was replaced by one or more other taxes.[53]

In fact, since adhesion to the WTO has opened the borders to much cheaper agricultural imports, government strategy seems to have changed. Probably because it feared the socially dangerous effects of a return to entirely private agriculture—the concentration of land for the benefit of a minority and the creation of a vast rural proletariat—the government confirmed its decision not to choose the dangerous solution of privatizing property, not just the use of the land, which would have made it possible to increase investments and make agriculture more competitive. And it seems to have found a way out: move three-quarters of the population in the countryside to cities to carry out the most important and profitable battle, industrialization. Later, in depopulated rural regions, it will perhaps realize its old dream, which was always to create large mechanized farms that it would privatize for the benefit of its best officials. As incredible as that may seem, the peasantry appeared to be living on borrowed time until some still timid measures were taken in the fall of 2008.[54]

Overall, although the great majority of incidents of social unrest are caused by abuses on the part of the powerful, they do not seem to be inspired by clear "class consciousness." And they do not seem very threatening to the authorities, because they are both short lived and localized. They often do not challenge the very widespread belief that impels many of the discontented to go to Beijing to voice their protest because the "center" of the regime, supposedly still virtuous, is the ultimate recourse.[55]

The Plutobureaucratic Class

But everything indicates that China is both dominated and directed by a plutobureaucratic class formed around money and power. "As in Russia," writes Lucien Bianco, "Djilas's 'new class' gave birth to a 'new new class,' which is recycling state property for its own benefit."[56] This class is essentially an outgrowth of the bureaucratic stratum that took shape after the CCP seized power in 1949 but whose cohesion had been damaged by the internal rectification campaigns and then by the Cultural Revolution. Although the first private entrepreneurs often seem to have come from outside this group, the group subsequently incorporated those who succeeded.[57] Later, a huge number of officials "dove into the sea" of business. Through their connections, they profited from the privatization of many state enterprises and the lax management of those that remained to develop their own companies. They then set up interest groups through family alliances and new friendships. But they have never abandoned their connections in the political and administrative apparatus. Indeed, the enormous power that the party-state maintains over the economy and the multifarious interconnections between the public and private sectors make those connections indispensable. This produces rich rewards for government officials, so that some particularly lucrative positions in the provinces are purchased, just as their counterparts used to be under the French monarchy.

This plutobureaucracy is thus twofold. It includes two populations united by a past, connections, and common interests—as well as, often, by blood ties. And there are more and more people wearing two hats. For example, whereas two-thirds of company heads are former communist officials, a growing number of them are, at the same time, like the CEO of Haier, the party secretary of their company, which makes things much simpler for them. Others have been appointed to important local positions, and, since 2005, former private company heads have been hired for management positions in the public sector.[58] Thus there are bosses but no employer class, as Frédéric Bobin writes; he goes on to show that the more prosperous and privatized the companies, the more the bosses accept the primacy of the state. It is unquestionable that they have every interest in doing so, because the financial and legal position of the head of a company is extremely precarious: the list of "very large fortunes" is constantly changing.[59]

The plutobureaucrats serve without hesitation the political and administrative hierarchies on which they depend. In every possible way, they create a "social envelopment" that helps control the population.[60] This envelopment is particularly apparent in provincial cities where the political leaders and businessmen meet with and collaborate with one another. The politicians, for example, supply administrative permits and police protection, and the businessmen keep the economy humming, ensure employment and work discipline, and provide supplemental income to their protectors and clients.

This upper fringe of Chinese society is worth comparing to the one that now controls postcommunist Russia. Though just as predatory, the Chinese version appears, however, to be more enterprising and to create more wealth, probably because its supporting political structure has also been firmer and more effective in carrying out its tasks. Through its economic activity and social influence, this fringe is perhaps *the* factor that has enabled the regime to change so many things while changing nothing, or giving that impression. It enjoys a twofold legitimacy that leaves no space for challenge: it brings together the masters of a national communism and the privileged players in a globalized capitalism, and it uses both the political and the economic tools of domination.

The Central Enigma of Post-Maoist China

There is more. The dual role, political and economic, of the dominant class no doubt helps explain why the power of the Chinese Communist Party has not—or not yet—died from the virus that monopoly has nourished within its ranks: the virus that prevented the regime from understanding difference and competing with it. Deng Xiaoping himself had, until the mid-1990s, merely adopted some capitalist procedures without also adopting the rules and modes of action that make capitalism profitable, organized, and civilized.

The situation has changed over the last ten years. To make their system more profitable, Chinese leaders purged the state sector and loosened the constraints holding back the private sector and foreign investment. To organize the private sector, they supplemented commercial law and applied it more strictly. To civilize it—that is, to reduce the suffering inflicted on workers and more generally on society as a whole—and thereby make their regime more durable, they inaugurated social policies, which were first focused on aid to the unemployed and gradually extended to other areas: old age, sickness, urban facilities, environment, culture. With the team of Hu Jintao and Wen Jiabao, this set of measures found its governing concept, the "harmonious society." The aim is now to move plutocratic authoritarianism toward a kind of social authoritarianism, or at least to put on that mask.

How is it that the most militant bureaucracy in the history of communism, the one that traveled the furthest in the totalitarian adventure, has changed into an opportunistic plutobureaucracy whose leaders have opened up to capitalist globalization and are cauterizing the wounds of their society? How can we understand the harmony that has been established between continuity and change, identity and difference? How are we to judge the fact that the leaders who still denounce the pernicious influences of Western "liberalism" are the same ones who soak up its technology and ideas? How is it that these nationalist ideologues commission study tours to countries around the world? Chinese newspapers have recently been discussing the Swedish model. And how are we to understand the fact that these gravediggers of freedom of thought are asking their intellectuals to explain globalization to them?

A review of communist history demonstrates the weak penetration of Marxism into a party that was primarily nationalist and military, a party that Mao Zedong terrorized rather than educating. Added to this was a strategic opportunism that Stalin immediately perceived and, further, the aptitude that communist cadres developed in the course of a long struggle to "recognize their failures and adapt to the circumstances," in which Lucien Bianco sees the primary reason for the victory of 1949.[61] I also believe there are reasons having to do with more recent history. First of all, the bureaucratic apparatus that followed Mao Zedong with difficulty was so shattered by the purge of the Cultural Revolution that after the storm anything was good in its view that would avoid the repetition of such an experience. Second and most important, thanks to Deng Xiaoping, the same apparatus took the plunge into business before—not after as in Russia—the fall of communism. Hence, its transformation into a plutobureaucracy took place under communist authority and to its advantage. This apparatus thus grew into a social class of apparatchiks and businessmen, a class clearly attached to communism—not as an ideology but as a system of power—but it was also able to study and listen to the capitalist world. It has undertaken a new course but has not identified completely with it, either because it remains also attached to the past or because it is already committed to a capitalist future. In sum, these plutobureaucrats are both the great strength and the great weakness of the Chinese regime.

Chapter 2

In a New World

UNLESS CHINA CHANGED ITS RELATIONSHIP WITH THE WORLD, strong growth would be inconceivable. Totalitarianism fostered the country's isolation: moving away from it implied opening up the society. And growth of the economy demanded that the country find in the outside world the necessary technical resources and commercial outlets. Opening to the world was thus the prelude to entering the world.

Entering the World

In the early days, the intention was only to open China to the world, and that only with extreme caution. This opening was primarily political and strategic; dealt with the economy only through governmental agreements, except for relations with the Chinese diaspora; and involved culture only in exchanges strictly controlled by official Chinese institutions. This caution lessened only slightly beginning in 1985, when Beijing began to recognize the positive character of the United Nations and undertook preparatory negotiations for China's entry into the WTO. This was a logical development: for one thing, domestic changes were slow to occur, and, for another, Chinese leaders understood the attraction that the democratic West held for the country's urban society during the years of the thaw.

It was precisely the contradiction between Chinese urban dwellers' attraction to the West and the despotic control maintained by the authorities, in a context of domestic inflation, that was the fundamental cause of the 1989 democratic insurrection. But its failure paradoxically allowed the authorities, without risk, to develop the role of the market and broaden the country's opening to Western economies and cultures, which got under way in 1992. When he designated Zhu Rongji to carry out this accelerated process, Deng Xiaoping told him bluntly: "The plan and the market are tools . . . they are not in themselves standards of capitalism or democracy."[1] A large and open call for foreign investments was launched; those investments would intensify technological gains, contribute needed financing, and allow the authorities to delay the development of private enterprise—that is, prevent the birth of a bourgeoisie.[2]

Should the country pursue this development to its logical conclusion and fully join an increasingly globalized world economy dominated by the United States, Japan, and Europe? That question was raised between 1997 and 1999. After a good deal of hesitation, the team of Jiang Zemin and Zhu Rongji decided to take the leap and moved the opening of the country into a third phase. The intention was now to integrate into the world as it was: Beijing was admitted to the WTO in November 2001. Moreover, to satisfy the policy's many opponents, immediate benefits were required: first came the award of the 2008 Olympic Games to Beijing, and this was followed by the profits from the triumph of Chinese exports. With Hu Jintao and Wen Jiabao, starting in 2002–2004, the turn became even more pronounced. Foreign policy now encompassed the political, economic, and even cultural domains, because the world was no longer only an external space but the very space within which China was developing, and therefore, China had to understand it fully. The first decade of the millennium comprised the years when the Chinese intelligence apparatus—in all senses of the term—most opened out into the world, whether to investigate the highest levels of American science and technology or to survey social policy in Europe.

This cautious and finally powerful integration of China into the world provokes contrasting thoughts. What is first apparent is the controlled, strategic, and even nationalistic character of the process. It was not engendered by a progressive conviction that this world was the only one possible and that it would turn out to be profitable, as well. Chinese leaders never lost sight of the tragic starting point of the development of modern China: the humiliations suffered and the mounting failures ever since the Opium Wars. And they never stopped relying on the most cynical convictions of the elites and the most xenophobic attitudes of the people. If you talk to canny Westerners living in Beijing, they will tell you about manipulated negotiations, the spying on their private life, and the bribes they have to pay if they are involved in an accident on the streets of Beijing. The "patriotism" instilled by primary education and maintained by propaganda is too insistent not to be intentional. China's first intention is to profit from the world. But it also intends to recover its ancient glory.

But once these concerns are expressed, one must acknowledge that their intensity is limited. On more important points, the opening to the world has now reached levels unforeseen and even unimaginable earlier on. Economically, of course, China's foreign trade has developed hugely since 1979, and its share of GDP—60 percent—has become essential, and half of Chinese exports are made by subsidiaries of foreign companies with branches in China.

For a time, there was a fear that the world into which China had just entered was in its view nothing but a gigantic market and a source of supply for resources. A stowaway on the ship of globalization, Beijing, it was claimed, exempted itself from any obligation or reciprocity. And indeed, suspicions and strategic interests for a long time were obstacles to the adoption of major international rules. But as China found advantages in doing so, it absorbed the humanitarian principles proclaimed by the Western powers and UN organizations. For several years, Chinese diplomacy has been developing in an increasingly "participatory" direction: it now provides more than two thousand peacekeeping forces, and the mercantile policies it had adopted at first with regard to Darfur and Burma have sometimes been modified. It has even collaborated in development aid programs. A borrower from the International Development Association until 1999, in December 2007 it participated in a $41.6 billion World Bank aid program for poor countries.[3] For Chinese elites, the world is now a place to explore and inhabit—and therefore defend: after making sure that the West would pay the principal costs, Beijing has joined most international campaigns for the protection of the environment. Chinese society has followed its elites in discovering the world from which it had so long been barred. Chinese tourism is no longer confined to a few nearby places such as Hong Kong, Thailand, and Singapore. It has spread to Europe, in the form of small, hurried groups, like the Japanese tourists of thirty years ago. In the first half of 2007, sixteen million Chinese went abroad, and this is only the beginning.[4]

Finally, a barely believable phenomenon is detectable in the country, a kind of ideological victory of the West. This may seem surprising at a time when people are hailing (or denouncing) the successes of Beijing, when the Chinese ruling class has asserted its firm allegiance to the regime, and when anger rumbles in the *hutongs* whenever national pride appears to have been insulted. Yet the duality of the regime and of its ruling circles authorizes both the persistence of nationalism or xenophobia and the at least temporary assimilation by those ruling circles of the values of globalization under the aegis of the West.

Did the Chinese simply want to make the right impression? Or are they totally sincere? Or both? Until the outbreak of the financial crisis in the fall of 2008, the elites and a significant portion of city dwellers had assimilated, in their own way, the three major beliefs that the West has been striving to legitimate around the world: globalization is fundamentally good (provided it benefits China), governance should be liberal in the economy and democratic in politics (provided China practices it in its own way), and individual freedom and modern comfort are decisive elements of happiness.

There is doubtless a distance between intentions and reality in a country that is still poor, where habits of violence persist, and whose regime intends to preserve its monopolies and pursue its predations for as long as possible—and for that purpose not shrinking from any abuse of language. But it must be acknowledged that the at least semantic victory of Western commonplaces over the celebrated "Chinese culture" that so many self-proclaimed experts in "intercultural dialogue" consider invincible has been spectacular. To take only one example, in 2006, Yu Keping, an assistant director of the most important research center of the CCP Central Committee, published a book bluntly titled *Democracy Is a Good Thing*.[5] He obviously enjoyed government protection, or he would not have utilized democratic terminology. But hadn't the official white paper on democracy published in the fall of 2005 set a goal for China of "political and social democracy"? Later, in March 2007, Wen Jiabao boldly declared that "socialism, democracy, and the rule of law are not mutually exclusive."[6]

The speech, of course, was in part a polite and sly salute of vice to virtue. But it tarnished the alleged success of a regime that, unlike its Soviet cousin, was supposed to have overcome the superiority of capitalism by playing at capitalism while *being* communist. The truth, on the contrary, is that if China has prospered, this is because it has agreed to abandon partially its own ideology and its own hopes to don the garb of globalization, because it understands that it has a future only through compromise and tinkering.

China's entry into the world seems to have taken the form of a kind of reciprocal assimilation: China assimilated the world and prepared to profit from it, but at the same time the world assimilated China to a degree unforeseeable a few decades ago. This process throws light on the domestic change that it also influenced. For just as the members of the Chinese ruling elite have assimilated the new grammar of the globalized capitalist economy, so they have been assimilated by it.

In a global situation of peace and economic growth, this process is a factor fostering stability, peace, and progress. China is no longer a disturbance to world order, and the world has become a decisive resource for the country's growth.

A Brilliant but Fragile Global Status

The policy of opening to the world has unquestionably been effective. Not only has it contributed a good deal to economic growth and hence to the stabilization of the regime, but it has secured outsized diplomatic results. China is indeed now among the major powers of the planet, although its economy remains in large part underdeveloped, its standard of living is generally low, and its army carries little weight in comparison to American and Russian forces.

Beyond the cleverness of its leaders, this exceptionally brilliant status is attributable to the fact that after a century and a half of being buffeted from the outside, the country has benefited from very favorable geopolitical circumstances. It profited a good deal from the anti-Soviet policies and then from the naïveté and shifts of American policy; the terrorist threat has now forced the United States to pay less attention to the Far East and hence to be less demanding of Beijing. In addition, as troubling as it may have been for the Chinese leadership, the collapse of the Soviet Union helped them by abolishing a strategic threat and opening Central Asia. The weaknesses and divisions of the European Union offered them room for maneuver that they were able to exploit brilliantly for commercial and technological purposes. Finally, the Asian economic situation worked in their favor. The two other regional powers could not rival Beijing: overdeveloped Japan remains diplomatically limited, and democratic India does not yet carry enough economic and strategic weight. Moreover, the Korean peninsula was becalmed by division, and Southeast Asia was slowly recovering from the Asian crisis. All this means that China now ranks high in the hierarchy of world powers, far behind the United States, of course, but at the level of the European Union and Russia. It has been able to use this very advantageous position by cleverly concealing the hesitations and divisions provoked in its ranks by the gradual abandonment of the opportunist line of the past in favor of a more responsible politics.

Yet the global status of China remains fragile in several respects. First and foremost, as I have noted, the country's worldwide influence depends a good deal on the naïveté and weakness of its competitors, which will not last forever. Beijing already finds itself in open conflict with its principal partners on three major issues: its aggressive trade policy and its refusal to quickly increase the value of the yuan; its human rights policy; and its environmental disasters, which threaten the ecology of the planet. These conflicts add an element of fragility to ongoing Chinese growth.

The primary weakness of the Chinese position, however, is domestic. It has to do with the fact that the opening is recent, which fosters internal debates and inconsistent policy choices. For example, Beijing's Japan policy has struggled to achieve balance because of the passions it stirs in public opinion and divergences at the highest levels. The position with respect to the United States is almost as fragile, but for somewhat different reasons: between China's unqualified admiration for the American model and its deep suspicion toward the world's major power is a contradiction that only time can resolve. But the principal contributor to the fragility of China's growth is the economic situation, particularly because the economy has an effect on foreign policy. It forces the state's foreign policy to act to protect supplies of raw materials, but economic concerns also supply it with increasingly powerful arguments by constantly strengthening the attractiveness of the Chinese market and the country's commercial and financial influence. An economic crisis or slowdown would greatly reduce these advantages and, at worst, reduce China to a lower rank, which in return could not fail to cast doubt on its policy of opening to the world.

Chapter 3

The Magnitude and Weaknesses of Growth

Jeffrey Sachs Applauds Chinese Growth

"CHINA IS THE GREATEST DEVELOPMENT SUCCESS THE WORLD has ever known."[1] This statement is one example of the widespread orthodoxy that considers Chinese growth to be extraordinary. Moreover, China's growth is sustainable, and China is thus destined to play the leading role in the world.

This argument is based primarily on the performance of the Chinese economy for nearly three decades. By accumulating annual growth rates of approximately 9 percent since 1980, the Chinese economy achieved a slightly better result than that of Japan in its best days and clearly better than that of South Korea subsequently. And—this is the most important point—China is an immensely larger and more populous country than these other two. The per capita GNP doubled between 1978 and 1986 and again between 1987 and 1996; calculated in purchasing power parity, per capita GNP ranked third in the world in 2007 and accounted for approximately 16 percent of world production, compared to approximately 20 percent for the European Union and the United States and a little less for the rest of Asia.

This growth brought about the modernization of the economy. The greatest portion of the economy is given over to industry and services, and its technical level is constantly improving, thanks to numerous borrowings from foreign technologies. China now produces automobiles and, as of 2009, civilian airplanes.[2] Growth also made possible an increase in per capita average income to nearly $1,000, which lifted four hundred million Chinese out of poverty. It at least doubled—from 20 to about 45 percent—the proportion of the population that is urbanized, which, according to the UNDP, could reach 70 to 80 percent between 2035 and 2040. It has transformed the participation of China in the world market: the country accounts for 12 percent of world trade, and in some months its exports exceed those of the United States. The world's largest importer of lumber, China now consumes close to half of the world's cement and has caused a continuous increase in the price of lead, among other commodities.[3]

It has thus become a major actor in the world market, thanks to record trade surpluses—$30 billion in September 2007 and $262 billion for the year—that it runs with the West, primarily the United States and Europe. Its foreign exchange reserves surpassed those of Japan in February 2006 and reached $1.52 trillion dollars at the end of 2007.[4]

This economy is relatively concentrated: 160 companies control 60 percent of China's GNP.[5] A few of them, long coddled by the government, have made a place for themselves in the world market, including TCL (televisions), Huawei (telecommunications), and Lenovo (computers). Several international markets have been crushed by Chinese exports, including toys, shoes, and microwave ovens.[6]

But the most impressive thing is what is supposed to be coming. Most observers believe that Chinese growth will continue at a sustained pace for a substantial period of time, which would turn the gradual emergence of the country into a veritable landslide and shift the center of the world economy to the Far East. This simultaneously optimistic and catastrophic prediction is justified by some or all of the following arguments: China has a huge population, which provides it both with a low-cost "reserve army" of migrant labor and an enormous potential market; it has an elite of high quality able to assimilate the advanced techniques imported from the West and even improve on them through rapidly growing research and development resources; its economy is regulated by a stable political regime and piloted by competent managers; it has the advantage of the dynamic environment of East Asia; and it receives regular infusions of Western investments.

These rational arguments are often mixed with another, less rational one—one that is not the least important to some observers: this economy represents an anti-West. Just as forty years ago "Mao Zedong thought" seemed to foreshadow the fall of a corrupt West, so the success of a low-cost Chinese economy seems to mean for some observers the revenge of work and discipline over a protected and lazy West.

What Growth Has Really Changed

Before articulating serious doubts about these predictions, I would like to point to what is true in Jeffrey Sachs's formulation.

It is certainly not the superlative: I do not find it possible to define an as yet incomplete process of development as "the greatest success the world has ever known." Nor is it the concept of "development," which says too much or not enough depending on the meaning it is given. The concept of "growth" seems more appropriate to designate a progression that is still indefinite in nature and has an unknown future. What is true is rather the justification of the importance of the event by the "knowledge" its participants and foreign partners had of it.

As incomplete as the effects of growth may be on the standard of living of the great majority of the Chinese, it has transformed not only their material conditions but, more deeply, their relations with the government. Communism freed individuals from their chains only to enslave them more harshly. Economic growth has conferred on them an economic value and a private freedom that many see as a kind of preparation for citizenship. Although it is not certain to lead the regime to rapid democratization, it is sure to favor the erosion of arbitrary power and to make increasingly necessary the construction of a modern state.

Just as important is the fact that Chinese growth has compelled the world to develop substantive relations with China and therefore to know more about it. China is now part, not of *its* world or *a* world, but of *the* world. That means that hostility has become less likely and cooperation increasingly possible. And, most important, it makes it possible to hope that events in China will unfold before the world's eyes, that other societies will make judgments about them, and that they will possibly intervene. Western leaders already have no hesitation in letting the Beijing authorities know what they think of their political differences, because the West is affected by them.

This new situation has produced two consequences. The first is that China now knows we are watching it and for that reason it has an interest in communicating a favorable image of itself. Before the Olympic Games, the city of Beijing offered free English classes to taxi drivers and demanded that the city's residents give up spitting and bare stomachs. To reduce pollution during the games, it limited automobile traffic.

For several years now, the Chinese leadership has been worried about what is "not fitting" in the country in the eyes of foreigners: prisons in the middle of cities, miserable or unpaid wages, counterfeit goods, corruption and bribery, forced eviction of residents, and so on. At first they tried to conceal these blots, but that was futile, because entry into the world market necessarily involved a massive presence of the foreign press. Then, beginning in 2004 and 2005, they undertook a second operation consisting of reducing these blemishes, first in large cities and then gradually in the rest of the country. Slums were removed from downtowns, then the prostitutes, soon to be followed by "hairdressers" discreetly awaiting their customers in their stalls. In the face of the scandal provoked by some dangerous exports, particularly toys, the Chinese government published a blacklist of the 429 companies that had violated existing export legislation and abolished the export licenses of more than seven hundred companies.[7] No one knows how far this conversion to "world standards" will go. One waits with particular interest for what will happen with Chinese counterfeit products, which account for two-thirds of the seizures by European customs authorities. But a process is unquestionably under way.

In return, it is probable that the world will be less passive if new tragedies happen in China. The authorities in Beijing can no longer refuse international aid, as they did during the Tianjin earthquake, which caused at least a half million deaths in July 1976. This was one of the regime's most scandalous crimes; the lives of thousands, perhaps tens of thousands, of people might have been saved. If famines were to occur, it is hard to imagine that they could last for four years, as happened from 1958 to 1962, before foreign partners send advice and assistance.

In other words, although not guaranteeing the best or providing assurances against the worst, the new relationship of China to the world makes more appropriate domestic policy and better external assistance—or vigilance—probable. The worst would not be prevented, but it would be limited by world public opinion.

"The Big One, Over There, in the Pool"

If one examines in a cold light the economic results achieved, it soon becomes apparent that many have exaggerated them and neglected their cost and precariousness.

Although China's economic results are considerable, those results are perceived as miraculous only because of two misperceptions. The first is that it is too often forgotten that China has a population of more than 1.3 billion, more than fifteen times the population of Germany, whose position it just recently overtook in the world economic hierarchy. Observers gloss over the fact that almost half the Chinese population lives on less than eight dollars a day, that the average income is one-thirtieth that of the French, and that the human development index places China eighty-ninth in the world.[8]

The second misperception is that many in the West imagine that the Chinese economy is entirely comparable to its most dynamic part, which is also its most visible: foreign trade, which has struck heavy blows against already faltering European industrial sectors such as textiles and shoes. But many are unaware of the fact that the majority of Chinese factories and practically all small local factories are technologically underdeveloped. In early 2007, one could still see delivery tricycles pedaling between the planes at the Shanghai airport. China remains a generally poor country, and extremely poor over the greater part of its territory: in 2004, only four coastal provinces had per capita annual incomes above €1000.[9] Pockets of poverty persist among the unemployed and the elderly urban population, and even more in the countryside of the most distant provinces least favored by nature: Shanxi, Gansu, Ningxia, Sichuan, Guizhou, and Guangxi.

In other words, the growth registered by the country for thirty years has not been enough to lift it entirely out of underdevelopment. Only a narrow minority of the Chinese have attained European living standards. Most of them are far behind and therefore do not have the means to obtain cultural goods and information resources. It should be added that many workers are still treated like slaves, particularly by companies that purchase laborers from the countryside and install them in what amount to private labor camps. Those workers suffer from every form of poverty.

Finally, China resembles an overgrown adolescent whose entry into a small swimming pool outrages other users. Because he is much bigger and fatter than the others and he stirs up a lot of water, he creates fear—yet, he still knows only the rudiments of swimming.

The Waste Associated with Growth

A second criticism has been made of China's form of growth: it has cost the country a good deal, and it continues to do so. As I noted earlier, the government, the members of the Communist Party, and the population are impatient, the first calculatedly and from political ambition, the second from greed, and the third because of a lack confidence. Hence, a choice was made in favor of very rapid growth, to the detriment of ecological precautions and the technological acquisitions that would have been necessary to take those precautions. This explains the considerable costs of Chinese growth.

First there is the waste. China uses seven times as much energy as Japan per unit of GDP, and has consumed 10 percent more energy every year since 2001. A goal had been set for 2006 to reduce energy consumption by 4 percent; it was not achieved. In addition, the Chinese economy devours 40 percent of the world's cement, 31 percent of the world's coal, and 27 percent of the world's steel. Coal mines are exploited without safety precautions, and underground fires consume two hundred million tons annually, almost four times French annual coal production at its peak.[10] Despite recent price increases, water is still one-third the price of the world average, which fosters waste and increases shortages, particularly in half of the cities: per capita water availability has been reduced to one-fourth the world average. In the great northern plains, the water table is dropping one meter each year, and some observers predict that agriculture will eventually have to be reduced or even abandoned to continue to supply the cities and industry.[11]

As for environmental pollution, the facts can be summed up in a catastrophic ranking: in 2006, China was ranked ninety-fourth out of 133 countries in the environmental performance index. The rank is in fact inaccurate, because if the area affected and the quantity of victims are taken into account, it should be placed even lower. The problem comes primarily from reckless industrial development devoid of any precautions and secondarily from equally thoughtless methods of heating (that is, using coal) and basic equipment. For example, the insulation and ventilation of dwelling units are highly inadequate in climates that are often extremely cold in winter and stifling in summer. Sixteen of the twenty most polluted cities in the world are Chinese, and the spectacle offered by some of them (for example Chongqing and Lanzhou, in their basins) is stupefying. One-third of rivers and streams are polluted, 190 million people suffer from ailments attributable to the consumption of contaminated water, and four hundred thousand die because of it every year. I have personally witnessed entire valleys polluted by factories, their villages populated by the mentally handicapped. It is estimated that

Chinese emissions of carbon dioxide will surpass those of the United States in 2009, in large part because China still derives 60 percent of its electricity from coal-fired plants. Industrial pollution is already costing the country between 8 and 12 percent of its GDP.

Coupled with chaotic urbanization, neglect of the environment has aggravated more general problems. For example, the region of Guangdong is threatened by rising water caused by climate change. Other problems are older: for example, two-thirds of the grasslands have been eroded, and the desert is increasing annually by 2,500 square kilometers.[12] The Beijing that I knew in the years between 2002 and 2007 reminded me of a stay in Tokyo in the early 1970s, with cloudless days but no sun and industrial odors so familiar that they turned into old friends.

In a sense, the comparison to Tokyo might make one optimistic, because the air in Tokyo is now purer than it is in Paris. But this came after huge public effort. The Chinese authorities have barely begun such an effort, seizing on the scandal caused by the poisoning of the Songhua River in the northeast in the fall of 2005. Over the years, the authorities have signed more than thirty conventions and treaties concerning protection of the environment and natural resources. They have established a budget of $175 billion for five years. The goal is to increase energy efficiency by 20 percent and reduce pollution by 10 percent by 2010.[13] The symbol of this strategic reversal was the official recognition, by its director, of the ecological risks created by the huge Three Gorges Dam, which was the great project of the Jiang Zemin regime.

The media have gradually taken up the ecological cause, which is popular in public opinion. Spectacular initiatives have been taken, such as the first day without automobiles organized in September 2007—unfortunately, it was held on a Saturday and scantily observed. But in most cases local authorities continue to encourage industrial production blindly. Although they have acquired clearer environmental awareness than in the past, they grasp the problem concretely only once they have reached a certain level of development.[14] Pan Yue, the brilliant deputy director of the State Environmental Protection Administration, recently stated that "the large polluting industries are protected by local governments," and an investigation of 529 companies located next to rivers and streams revealed that 44 percent of them were violating the law.[15]

As a matter of interest, I might mention a final type of familiar waste, the vague complex of clientelism, corruption, and embezzlement that costs between 3 and 6 percent of Chinese GDP.[16] In fact, this unquestionably real phenomenon is subject to exaggeration and simplification. Its magnitude in China is exaggerated, while it is forgotten that it is found in many other countries undergoing rapid development—the countries of Europe experienced it during the period of their industrial takeoff. And it is simplified by giving it a cultural definition (the famous Chinese system of *guangxi*, "relations"), whereas it often designates the predatory activity of a social class or is a response to the need to escape from archaic regulations. Although it is costly to the current Chinese economy, it served that economy in a delicate transition phase, when what was important was to engage the country, and particularly its ruling party, in a new type of economy. Corruption was the price to be paid to push the CCP personnel into the new era, which explains the complete difference from the failed transition in the Soviet Union.

But it is obvious that to complete its integration into the world and to stabilize the functioning of its economy, China will have to get rid of at least the most visible and largest scandals, because they demoralize the population and nourish its contempt for its leaders. For example, the highway companies secure vast territories for free and then sell plots at exorbitant prices,[17] and construction companies exploit labor and materials to their utmost limits: for instance, in the fall of 2007, a female student at the lycée français in Beijing was crushed when a crane collapsed.

The Four Swords of Damocles

"Agriculture is both the foundation and the weak link of the Chinese economy," according to the economist François Gipouloux.[18] Its primary problem is insufficient profitability, which places it at risk in the face of the foreign imports authorized by China's entry into the WTO.

In addition, 30 to 40 percent of agricultural laborers are more or less unproductive. The central authorities approach the question from a social angle, promising decreases in taxation rarely applied by the local authorities, because the provincial authorities in charge of agriculture are chiefly concerned with industrial development. The ending of state intervention in the production and marketing of most agricultural products seems to have had no dynamic effect. Indeed, the heart of the problem is political: until Beijing abolishes state ownership of land, property will remain fragmented, the peasants will have no access to bank credit, and agriculture will remain separate from the modern economy.[19]

The state industrial sector also continues to pose serious problems, despite the purge it went through in the 1990s. In spite of an attempt to focus around a few pilot companies, many companies have dubious claims to profitability. State companies facing financial risk were simply excluded from the bankruptcy law that went into effect in June 2007.[20] In fact, these companies are so necessary for employment and so protected by provincial authorities that the banks (most of which are in the public sector) maintain them on life support, to the detriment of the private sector (which they do not support) and their own balance sheets. These loans "between comrades," which are impossible to repay, constantly reopen the wound that appeared in the 1990s: the extreme fragility of a banking system paralyzed by bad debts, in spite of "defeasance" procedures that have already contributed $450 billion dollars. Despite recent regulations requiring agreement by the central government for any new loan, bad debts are believed to still amount to between 20 and 40 percent of GDP. Hence, it is not an exaggeration to say that the Chinese banking system is technically insolvent.[21]

And the stock exchange system is no better. Loaded with archaic and bizarre practices—two-thirds of the listed companies are not tradable—it has developed in a strange and exaggerated way: very low from 2001 on, then peaking after the 2005 reform, creating a speculative bubble. Significantly, rumors about government interventions provoked various troubling movements in the spring of 2007: the stock market has little affection for the political authorities.[22] But the inflation that arrived the following summer worsened the problem, because by exceeding the interest on bank deposits it drew tens of millions of Chinese into the stock markets. The Shanghai market index has more than tripled since 2005, and by May 2007 the value of shares traded on Chinese exchanges exceeded that of shares traded on other Asian exchanges, including those of Japan. Subsequently, prices continued to rise to completely artificial peaks, which makes financial analysts fear the worst.[23] What will happen with this fever? What will be the effects of the world stock market crisis that began in January 2008? No one knows, but international financial circles are on the alert.

These banking and stock market failings make the other weaknesses connected to the influence of the international economic situation on the Chinese economy even more dangerous. The condition of the economy is such that the country would perhaps not withstand a crisis comparable to the one that affected all of Asia in 1987. The Chinese economy, once so closed, is now more open—its primary protection is the fact that the yuan is still not convertible. The economy is dependent on raw materials, particularly minerals (China accounts for more than one-third of world imports) and oil—Beijing has to import 40 percent of its consumption.[24] Up to now it has maneuvered rather well in this area, notably through a strong African offensive that has changed who its traditional suppliers are. But prices are constantly rising, and China lives through its competitiveness. In the alleys of Beijing and Shanghai, people are wondering: what will become of us when the price of a barrel of oil goes above $200?

A second set of short-term dependencies are related to trade surpluses with Western markets, particularly the American market. In response to protests from Washington, the Beijing authorities reduced the surplus from 31 to 22.7 percent in 2006.[25] But this is still too high for their trading partners. More important, it is too high in the view of the Chinese leaders, who pay close attention to the world economic situation and have long feared the consequences of a deterioration of the American economy. They are quite aware that an annual reduction of 1 percent in American economic growth would produce a 0.5 percent reduction in Chinese growth.[26]

And it is precisely from a mishap in America that the Chinese leaders fear will come a dangerous sequence of events that will accentuate the weakness of their banks. They have therefore had the time to prepare. Moreover, the Chinese state has the resources to pursue a strong recovery policy. It is still true that a massive capital flight would be slowed by the inconvertibility of the yuan. It is also true that the country has accumulated colossal foreign reserves. The worst is not certain, but it is also not impossible. The economy is both the basis for the new stability and what threatens it. It is the triumph of the regime and what puts it in danger.

Book II

The Acid Test

Chapter 4

Explanation

THE FORAY INTO THE CHINESE ECONOMY THAT I AM ABOUT TO embark on is inspired by my experience as a pedestrian in the alleys of Beijing, the *hutongs*. Over the course of five years, this experience has enabled me to supplement and qualify the economic analyses that were current at the time, because it provided me with a more concrete view of the human factors governing Chinese growth.

These factors are not cultural constants but aspects of the contemporary "Chinese moment." Their importance comes in particular from the fact that they help explain both the practically universal increase in the costs of production and the emergence of a new and even more costly challenge, which implies a change in economic policy.

The Universal Increase in Costs

The belief is common in the West that Chinese growth somehow bene-fits by definition from very low costs. This is no longer completely true and, more important, it is becoming less and less so.

China is relatively poorly endowed with natural resources. It has abundant coal for the production of energy. But what was once an advan-tage is now its misfortune, because the resulting pollution is so dangerous. Coal use has to be reduced, but hydropower and nuclear power, which together produce 3 percent of the country's energy, are not sufficient. China thus relies on oil, but its supply is limited, so it must import almost half of what it consumes. And all it takes is a colder than average winter, like that of 2007–2008, for there to be electricity shortages, creating an apocalyptic atmosphere.[1] Even more imports would thus be required to build up reserves. Comparable tensions arise with respect to many other mineral resources, and China's massive consumption of them has pushed up world prices. And the Chinese economy devours more than one hun-dred million cubic meters of wood annually.[2]

The supply of raw materials is one of the most serious concerns of the Chinese leadership. New sources of supply constantly have to be found, if possible far from the mayhem in the Middle East: since 2004, Africa has become its core source. But friendship with these new suppliers has to be kept up and future supplies guaranteed. For example, it was learned in the spring of 2007 that China intended to provide $20 billion to Africa over the next three years to finance trade and infrastructure.[3] But there are also political costs to having to protect the bloody dictatorships of Sudan and Burma at UN meetings.[4]

At least low labor costs were until recently considered to be the immense advantage of the Chinese economy. But this period is coming to a close. It is little known in the West that Chinese wages are rapidly ris-ing, and at an increasing rate. Local authorities sometimes rein this move-ment in, whereas the Beijing government cautiously approves it and has also adopted increasingly protective labor laws, whose effects will be costly when they are more fully applied. These laws come in response to economic as well as social causes. They are designed to expand the role of consumption and to encourage the economy to produce more expensive consumer goods.

Reliable statistics were lacking, because it was important not to discourage investors. In any event, I remember that when I arrived in Beijing in the spring of 2002, average wages were officially just above 700 yuan, and when I left five years later they had reached nearly 1,400 yuan, whereas prices had risen only modestly in that period. This memory has been corroborated by various sources that estimate wage increases to have been between 14 and 20 percent annually in recent years.[5] These figures were confirmed by Japanese analysts, who estimated, with some exaggeration, that labor was twice as expensive in the coastal regions of Fujian and Guangdong as it was in Vietnam, where Chinese companies had relocated.[6] Banking sources consider China to be the Asian country that experienced the largest wage increase in 2007: 16.7 percent compared to 16 percent in India.[7] In fact, labor costs vary greatly depending on location; they are higher in developed regions and much lower in the interior provinces.

In addition, the circumstances of migratory workers were in the process of changing. Economists were for a long time right to see them as a "reserve army" of labor for the Chinese economy. Indeed, it was this labor force—now between 150 and 200 million—that made Chinese factories so attractive because of their low wages. It was long believed that, because of the huge reserve of rural migrants—still several hundred million workers—the cost of their labor would increase little or not at all.[8] Yet the development seems clearly to have accelerated since the gigantic boycott of the Guangdong and Fujian factories in 2004–2006 that forced foreign companies to pay each employee 1,600 yuan (€160) monthly, including food, lodging, and insurance.[9] The information available indicates wage increases in this case as well ranging between 15 and 20 percent annually since 2005 and more than doubling in five years at Beijing construction sites. Wages sometimes come close to those of regular workers, and migrants in Guangdong have begun to negotiate their working conditions.[10] Since the policies of the central authorities favor the establishment of minimum wages in the provinces—780 yuan or €78 per month in Guangdong, an increase of 14 percent in December 2006[11]—and encourage the signing of contracts with worker protection clauses and the standardization of working conditions, it is likely that this development will continue and even accelerate in the coming years.

The increase in wage costs is a response to fundamental conditions that will remain in effect in the future, even if Chinese wages remain comparatively low. The first condition is that at present in China workers are as grasping and rebellious with regard to wages as the rest of the population. The second is that the compartmentalization of the territory of China often creates tensions in the labor market. In a few years, this factor will be intensified by the effect of birth control on the age pyramid, which will reduce the number of newcomers to the labor market: China, as we shall see, will become an aged country before it becomes a developed one.

This increase in ordinary labor costs has become better known since 2006 and has been the subject of major reports in the Western press, including the French regional press.[12] Observers often add other related costs: the nearly Western wages of upper-level technicians, engineers, and accountants; the volatility of the qualified workforce; the complications and costs of starting a business in China; increased real estate prices; and the inflation of consumer prices. In short, China is becoming expensive in the view of companies that turned to it exclusively for its low costs. The price of goods exported to the United States in 2007 is estimated to have increased by 2.4 percent, and that is beginning to be known. A survey by Capgemini indicates that this new perception has strengthened the attraction of competing destinations, such as Vietnam, Cambodia, and especially India.[13]

A second series of costs depends more directly on official policy: these are the costs of social and cultural equipment, costs that are likely to amount to huge sums. Until recently, this equipment was often simply forgotten about in the construction programs of new developments, as though it was thought that individuals and local municipalities would work things out later. For example, the leaders of a delegation of French real estate agencies told me in the spring of 2006 of their stupefaction at the "naked" development sites they had visited: no gardens, no schools, no big stores, no clinics, no movie theaters. The private sector and the informal economy probably filled in some of the gaps later, particularly when it came to stores and restaurants. And local officials try to stimulate initiatives to set up "civilized neighborhoods" and provide for green spaces. But that is not enough. And contrary to what one may think from a distance, the notorious Chinese social "difference" does not take care of everything, for there are already signs of desocialization on the outskirts of large cities: theft, brawling, punctured tires, poisoned pets, and so on. It is this situation that is driving the authorities to act, and it will cost them dearly.

In addition, at the other end of China, in the most distant countryside, almost everything remains to be done: building all-weather paved roads, developing water resources, immediately reforesting eroded areas, developing towns and villages, building a minimum of public facilities such as clinics, rebuilding schools. All these problems have to be faced simultaneously, and all of them require finances. Until now, local authorities thought they could finance costs through fees or the establishment of "development zones" for private companies. That will obviously not be enough, and localities will inevitably turn to provincial authorities that have so far concentrated on the most profitable large operations.

A third category of costs are those for social policies. This is probably the primary focus of the team of Hu Jintao and Wen Jiabao. It is largely on their action in this area that they will be judged. Social policy has economic justifications, because it might play an essential role in the necessary stimulation of domestic consumption. But at the present time, it also responds to a strong popular aspiration for the prosperity of the 1980s, which is probably what the Chinese population chiefly expects from its leaders. And the expectation is easily understandable. Peasants have suffered harshly from economic ups and downs, and more than half of them have no means of paying for health care. Many of them can do nothing if they have an accident. Others pay as long as they can and then give up; there is, for example, the story of a migrant family that had spent all its savings to treat the mother for a cerebral hemorrhage and then brought her to the local crematorium still alive.[14] Since the collapse of work units, the diminution of the public sector, and the spread of insecure employment contracts, the majority of the urban population—57 percent according to the Shanghai Academy of Social Sciences—lacks any social safety net.[15]

As always, the first steps by the authorities were taken in cities—city dwellers receive 80 percent of social welfare payments. At first, beginning in the mid-1990s, the authorities started to deal with the most urgent problem, unemployment, through a gradual and very diversified institutionalization of the category of the *xiagang* (literally, "those who stepped down from their posts"), which gave rights to assistance and connections to the company.[16] This system, whose advantages varied depending on the intensity of social unrest in various localities, has often been replaced since early in the 2000s by financial assistance or the payment of some years of social security taxes.

The desire to avoid danger is also visible in the treatment of the large-scale poverty that appeared with mass unemployment: there were fifty million of the "very poor" in 1998.[17] For the urban portion of this new category, the authorities instituted a minimum income payment, the *dibao*; the names of its recipients—20.5 million in 2003[18]—are posted in every neighborhood so everyone can participate in monitoring their poverty.

But public opinion is obviously awaiting long-range measures dealing with health insurance and retirement: 70 percent of the Chinese population is worried about retirement.[19] With the number of beneficiaries of the old system of work units constantly decreasing, the authorities have gradually implemented insurance systems, at first as experiments. But in 2005 the new form of health insurance covered only 76 million urban employees. Moreover, 80 percent of the new retirement system consists of capitalized savings and therefore usually provides little to retirees. In all, 30 percent of the Chinese population over sixty has one kind or another of retirement income, but only 10 percent have health insurance.[20]

To be fair, it should be acknowledged that the Chinese regime in this instance has opened the way to the establishment of real social policies and has unquestionably sought effectiveness. But the efforts made so far seem very insufficient to a population made demanding by the rapid rise in its living standards and the information it has available about developed countries. The authorities will have to do more, more quickly. In any case, the necessary expenses will be colossal.

And they are likely to grow even larger in the future because of coming demographic changes. The Chinese population will quickly grow older. This tendency is the inevitable effect of the harsh birth control policy adopted in the early 1970s: the generations born in the 1950s and 1960s will not be entirely replaced. Up to 2020, the population over sixty will grow five times faster than the population as a whole, and by 2050 the ratio of workers to retirees will decline from 5 to 1 to 2 to 1. In Shanghai, the proportion of those over sixty is expected to increase from 20 percent today to 33 percent in 2020.[21] In other words, more and more Chinese will need insurance as fewer and fewer young workers will be engaged in the production of wealth.

The Tragedy of Health Care

The needed reforms include an urgent and essential task: the construction of a real health care system. In the absence of this, other social policies will be meaningless. At present, health care conditions are the shame of a China that still calls itself a people's republic. It is also one of the main reasons for the excess savings that are retarding the development of a real consumer market. First and foremost, this is because of the number of ailments caused by the stagnation and sometimes decline of public hygiene. A few figures: of 320 million smokers, 1.2 million die annually as a consequence of their addiction; 130 million Chinese carry the hepatitis B virus; 200 million suffer from illnesses related to their working conditions; 4.4 million have tuberculosis; and 1.5 to 2 million suffer from AIDS, a large portion of them because of trafficking organized by local authorities.[22]

Moreover, the hospitals that are supposed to treat these diseases fail in most of their duties. This is first because, receiving ever less support from public budgets (the state's share of health expenses has fallen from 32 percent in 1978 to 18 percent in 2005),[23] they have become scarcer where the need is greatest, in rural areas, where the number of beds has declined by 16 percent since 1982. Forced to pursue profit first of all, they are living essentially off the sale of often adulterated medicines or by exaggerating the number of tests they require of their patients. There are anecdotes everywhere in China of patients who come in for a sore throat being forced to undergo gynecological exams, of completely unnecessary Cesareans, and the excessive use of antibiotics that result in terrible epidemics. I have my own story: having consulted a doctor about my lung problems, in January 2004 I was told I most likely had cancer, a diagnosis that, after verification in France, turned out to be imaginary.

In addition, hospitals are so expensive that patients from the country abbreviate their stays. The rich also do not always have confidence in the "red envelopes" they give to doctors: for some years Hong Kong has been besieged by Chinese of the privileged class, who think it is safer to give birth in the former colony.[24]

The result of this collection of irresponsible actions and dishonesty is scandalous. People with few resources rely on magical cures and so-called Chinese medicine, which allows a cancer patient to die in a few weeks.[25] During the SARS epidemic, official television broadcast advertisements for creams that promised "eternal" protection. In all, the number of Chinese with access to public health is estimated to have declined from 71 percent in 1981 to 21 percent in 1993. Whereas the standard of living has enormously risen over the last three decades, life expectancy as of 2005 had increased by only three and a half years, half as much during the same period as in Hong Kong, Singapore, and South Korea, where the starting point was higher.[26]

A New Challenge

The reform of the health care system is a necessary component of the social policies that the Chinese authorities have to bring to fruition. It is also an essential element of a second, even more costly challenge, one that is making a decisive contribution to the definition of the contemporary Chinese moment. This challenge goes well beyond the already difficult effort the Beijing authorities have undertaken to keep both the Chinese economy and their own regime afloat. It is intended to lift their country to the highest or, more precisely, the most appropriate level.

Bernard Debré, a former French government minister and noted urologist who has frequently cooperated with a Shanghai hospital, once summarized the problem for me in this way: "They have some excellent hospitals, but they will become truly modern only when they construct a real health care system." And the second challenge that the Chinese authorities have taken up is precisely the challenge of modernity, that is, the gradual achievement of parity with the most developed and civilized nations.

To understand the genesis of this challenge, we have to come back to Deng Xiaoping in 1978–1979. He knew what he did not want: to abandon Leninist organizational principles or return to Maoist madness and misery. He knew what he wanted for the short term: to unleash real economic growth. But beyond that, he knew only vaguely where he wanted to lead China, and he deciphered the answer only gradually and cautiously, because his approach was so novel and dangerous. Roughly, he was inclined to look to the Western countries while not losing sight of the regime's capacity for absorption and the reactions of the various components of the leadership. He used this image: "To cross the river, you have to feel the stones."

In a sense, both despite and because of this ability to endure uncertainty, a first acid test was victoriously passed in the years from 1979 to 2000. The regime was gradually able to detach itself from Maoism. Second, it was generally able to define "the stones" on which to put its weight: basically, economic growth and confidence in the CCP. And third, it ventured rather far into the river, far enough to place China in the current of globalization driven by the capitalist countries.

But the path traveled raised a series of questions that formed a new challenge, the challenge of modernity, of the highest level to be attained. The first and most urgent question was that of competitiveness or economic modernity. The issue was no longer just to achieve growth but to do so in the most profitable sectors, which meant intensifying all the inputs: scientific and technical cooperation, technological espionage and purchases, the return of graduates from the United States, and the development of indigenous research capacities.

The second question was the question of social modernity. The Chinese leaders understood that a modern economy cannot exist without an equally modern society, and thus, as they said with the paternalism of engineers of human souls, it was necessary to elevate the "quality" of the Chinese population to build a "harmonious society." Health, sport, culture, collective ethics, and especially public policy then became the decisive elements.

The third, political, question has been, as Yves Chevrier writes, the Ariadne's thread of Chinese history since the Opium Wars. The question has evolved in recent times, first because the totalitarian solution was eliminated by the Maoist catastrophe and further because the dominant idea is now that a government derives its authority largely through the exercise of new responsibilities, among which are social justice and strict legality. How do these new responsibilities fit into the dogma? The answer is not very clear, and propaganda deals with it with ambiguous expressions. But a series of television programs on "the rise of the great powers" broadcast in early 2007, with the support of the highest authorities, focused on the decisive role played by "the primacy of law and the state." In short, there was a kind of implicit debate extending the responsibilities of the party-state to ever nobler spheres.

Resuming Control Over Growth

The policy of the "four modernizations" adopted in the past by Deng Xiaoping has changed into a policy of the construction of modernity. The goal is specified in demands that are both concrete and urgent: put an end to the waste created by the exclusive focus on exports, stimulate the birth of a domestic market, and move into high-quality production through technical improvements and social harmonization. But the condition for carrying out this new policy is the restoration of central control over growth and, especially, slowing its pace. Indeed, the frantic pace of growth since China's entry into the WTO has been based on the priority given to exports and on a remarkably high level of investment—almost 40 percent of GDP—which together have caused a good deal of waste, limited domestic consumption, and subjected the economy to serious external risks. Chinese and foreign economists agree on the diagnosis: if the Chinese economy continues galloping at this rate, sooner or later it is in danger of disaster. Jiang Zemin had been held back from acting by the racketeering of his Shanghai supporters. But Hu Jintao and Wen Jiabao have been ritually sounding the alarm since Jiang lost his last leadership post in the spring of 2004. On December 8, 2006, commenting on a "central committee meeting on economic work," the *Beijing News* headlined: "Next year, the economy will be asked first to do better and then to go more slowly." Since then, appeals to reduce the rate of growth have multiplied, especially in sectors that consume the greatest quantity of raw materials.

But up to early 2008, all these appeals have had a result that is hard to believe: not only did the rate of growth not slow, but it increased from 10.7 percent in 2006 to 11.4 percent in 2007, which indicates much higher numbers in coastal regions.[27] What happened? Especially, what happened to make the Chinese government suddenly so weak? Something very simple: the government did not have the means to impose its policy. Precisely because the policy was on target, it gave rise to a powerful coalition of interests against it that included all of the provincial authorities, themselves driven by their subordinate levels, as well as by Chinese and foreign business circles.

This is hardly surprising. After all, the central authorities demanded of local authorities in the first place that they ensure economic development and full employment. And the center had organized the privatization of a large part of the economy, encouraged foreign investment throughout the country, and closed its eyes to the multifarious connections between the economic world and political leaders at every level. Moreover, if local and provincial officials dragged their feet in response to the center's appeals to reason, this was because they knew their rank and file very well. They knew that the absolute condition for the loyalty of the plutocrats and the obedience of the general public was the maintenance of very rapid economic growth. There thus developed in the party apparatus a very simple message passed on to the central leadership: do whatever you want, but don't interfere with the pace of growth.

And some in the leadership were particularly inclined to listen to this message. First were the former associates of Jiang Zemin who were still very powerful in the Politburo. They were followed by a number of former provincial officials who had been promoted to the Politburo. Hu Jintao himself had governed Guizhou and Tibet in the 1980s, and his two likely successors, Xi Jingping and Li Keqiang, have also just left provincial posts.

Hence, a debate that in a democratic regime would have led to the formation of two rival camps is developing within a single political apparatus that holds the monopoly of power. As long as Hu Jintao did not control all the levers of power, that is, from 2004 to 2007, he operated in a cautious manner that favored the supporters of existing positions. At the very least, propaganda campaigns prepared people's minds. Some used the pretext of local scandals, mining accidents, pollution, corruption, or sexual excesses. Others were motivated by foreign expressions of dissatisfaction, for example with the bad quality of Chinese products. The situation changed to an extent that is not yet clear when the Seventeenth Congress of the CCP in October 2007 ratified Hu Jintao's political line and granted him more power, although not removing the hostile clans with whom he still has to negotiate.

The Confrontation Between Two Lines

In fact, two tendencies were in a muffled confrontation, the one that had held power and the other that was now in power and wanted to exercise it more fully. There was also a personal conflict. Hu Jintao is both a colder personality and more concerned with popular aspirations than Jiang Zemin; conversely, Wen Jiabao does not have the look of a high official like his predecessor Zhu Rongji, and he sometimes adopts a compassionate style.[28] But the difference between the two lines is also explained by the discontinuity between the two recent periods of Chinese history, that of the entry into globalization and the following period, in which, after the success of the first, the issue is to care for the poor and foster mature growth. The period of the Shanghai men was followed by that of the men from Beijing, who favored a port that was closer and easier to control, Tianjin.

The first line, still followed more or less clearly by many provincial leaders, is the one that ruled until the early 2000s. Globalist and business oriented, it attributes great importance to the labor-intensive export industries. This has been the source of China's recent economic triumph as well as of its wastefulness and weaknesses. In a sense, it represents the second age of the post-Maoist Chinese economy.

In contrast, the line Hu Jintao has laid out since he forced Jiang Zemin to leave the stage in 2004 and whose adoption he imposed in October 2007 is both more ambitious and more difficult to implement. It outlines what could become a third age. The issue is not to develop trade connections with the world but to master them in order to sharpen them. Nor is there a question of producing more but rather of producing better products, to blaze a trail toward the technological vanguard. No longer is it a question of increasing the country's new power but rather of making it technologically, socially, and ecologically sustainable.

Significantly, this political line emerged for the first time in an affair that involved public health. It arose from a major act of negligence by the Jiang Zemin clan, which was still powerful, at the time of the SARS epidemic in the spring of 2003, a mistake that produced a major shakeup in the Beijing municipal government, which Jiang had previously controlled. In 2004, after Jiang had resigned in the spring from the chairmanship of the Central Military Commission of the CCP, the first calls for cooling off the economy were heard. This line was later manifested during the fall of 2004 through an ideological crackdown, which was a way both of reassuring the regime's conservatives and of showing that the country should not exhaust its vitality in its relations with the world and the West. And beginning in the fall of 2005, thanks to the scandal of the pollution of the Songhua River, the new line was fully implemented in advocating cleanup of the pollution, a recognition of the people's difficulties, the rule of law, social policies, community development, and public transportation—and by delivering repeated criticisms of abuses of every order committed by local representatives of the party-state. Provincial and local officials were now to be judged not solely on their capacity to develop production and attract foreign investment but also on new criteria: reduction of inequality, protection of the environment, political stability, and their ability to practice the principles of democracy and the rules of legality.[29] The new line was thus both more "modern" and more sensitive to popular aspirations, at least as they were expressed by the urban population. In this sense, there is some connection to the Maoist training that the young Hu Jintao received in the early 1960s, when he was a member of the vanguard of the Communist Youth League at Qinghua University.

This new political line also exuded a whiff of nationalism. For some time, measures have been taken to force foreign companies to apply the rules the Chinese authorities set for them more strictly: for example, Wal-Mart has been forced to accept the organization of unions (official, of course) in its sixty Chinese stores.[30] The tax advantages foreign companies enjoyed have been abolished, and the sectors in which they can operate have been more strictly limited. Controls on foreign residents have been strengthened, and in November 2007 the Beijing police transformed a drug crackdown into an anti-African roundup.

Fewer precautions are taken with foreigners, because they are considered to be closely enough connected to the Chinese economy but also because the central authorities have given priority to domestic modernization in the broad sense of that term. This is the underlying principle of the new policies, and it would be a mistake to ignore this ambition. Libraries are proliferating in the large cities. The brand-new Beijing library, which is huge and modern, is a real cultural center, with a video library, film screenings, and lectures—I remember that in the spring of 2006, it presented a lecture intended for women who wanted to "master their bodies."

So Hu Jintao and Wen Jiabao have high ambitions. They intend to construct a high-level economy whose power would be based not only on low production costs and exports of cheap goods but on an advanced level of technology, a strong domestic market, and the export of high-value-added products, that is, a social, cultural, and technological modernity. The goal is to follow, as quickly as possible, the path already taken by the Japanese and Korean economies.

That's not all. The Beijing regime now intends to accomplish what other communist regimes failed to and what China itself was unable to do in 1989: survive not through repression but by taking hold of the economic, social, and cultural advantages of the democratic enemy. In China, it is not democracy that would flourish from the contributions of socialism, but communism would be strengthened by the contributions of the social democracies. There can be no doubt that we are facing the most convincing attempt to perpetuate a communist regime by reconciling it with the rules of the most modern societies.

The Cost of the High-End Market

Assuming it is applied, the new political line, however, has one defect: it further increases the already anticipated rise of all costs. An excellent example is the training of a more qualified work force. This is obviously indispensable, because "in the absence of qualified workers, China risks appearing to foreign investors as merely an offshore assembly platform."[31] In 2006, for example, the country needed three hundred thousand accountants but had only sixty-nine thousand. It also had a shortage of well-trained lawyers and engineers as well as of intellectually and linguistically international managerial staff. It will also have to train 2,200 airline pilots annually for the next decade.[32]

Chinese managers will also have to assimilate foreign techniques more thoroughly. Often brilliant progress has been made, to be sure. This usually finds expression in an explosion of industrial counterfeiting, for example in automobiles: all Western brands have been more or less directly copied, and the results of these hybrids are starting to be exported. The German high-speed train is also being studied. As for Airbus, it is said in China that one of those purchased is in the process of being taken apart. There is a saying in Shanghai: "We can copy everything except your mother."

Chinese excesses in this area have provoked legitimate anger around the world. But they should not mask the real situation, which Erik Izraëlewicz defines accurately: "Chinese high tech is neither high nor Chinese."[33] To begin with, the general technological level is still low. In addition, copying itself is an obvious sign of backwardness, and while the Chinese are striving to copy, Western research is moving forward.

The Case of Education and Research

This situation is no doubt temporary; in principle, there is no reason why China should fail where Japan succeeded. But it will have to pay the same price as Japan to modernize its system of education and research. Beijing's system now receives only 3 percent of the state's budget. Its base was weakened by the devolution of education to local authorities, which are often crushed by debt. The quality of teaching therefore declined, and student absenteeism has become a scourge in the countryside, particularly for girls. The illiterate population grew from eighty-six to 116 million between 2000 and 2005, an astonishing development.[34] Secondary education is extremely uneven, particularly because private schools have proliferated.

As for the university system, it has progressed enormously compared to the past and now has twenty-four million enrolled students. A minority of elite universities receive considerable funds from the state and are trying to advance in international rankings. But there is a problem of quality even in these universities—not so much of the students, who have gone through a rigorous selection process and work unstintingly, but of the professors, who teach in a uselessly authoritarian manner and often have only a vague idea of the level of knowledge required in the West. Matters are even worse for the administration, which is recruited on political and bureaucratic rather than professional criteria. And the system does not meet market demand: the education, not always up to date and not very practical, does not foster mobility, particularly internationally. The students know this, and that is why the best of them have gone to the West and recently to Hong Kong and Australia as well.[35]

As for the research system, it has also made enormous progress compared to the past, but, with the exception of a few sectors, it cannot be compared to its Western counterparts. Research and development expenses grew from 0.6 percent of GDP in 1995 to 1.5 percent in 2005, and they continue to increase annually by 20 percent. This is enough to make some enthusiasts optimistic, even overly so. Moreover, although foreign companies compete in claiming satisfaction with their Chinese research and development centers—there were seventy-five in 2006, most charged with technical adaptations[36]—how many of them have hired a Chinese researcher for their own research staff? The number of patents filed by Chinese, outside international cooperative ventures, remains small. Basic research is often neglected, and some essential areas remain very weak. In addition, Chinese research is notorious for its many scandals: half the theses are copied or bought, and China, which is ranked fifth in the world in the number of theses produced, is ranked only 120th for their quality. And 70 percent of companies simply do not have a research and development department.[37]

So if the Chinese authorities want to develop and modernize universities and research, they cannot be satisfied as they have been until now with concentrating resources on a small number of elite institutions and allowing the others to increase their tuition fees. They will have to consolidate the entire educational system, improve teacher training and the teaching of foreign languages, and distribute resources and increase quality controls throughout the university and research system. They will also have to improve pedagogy and professionalize university administration, improve research ethics, systematically foster methodological skills and independent thinking among students, provide real university careers, and favor innovation. This is quite a program. The cost of better university training and more innovative research will be huge not only in financial terms but also ideologically and politically.

Take the example of the most brilliant students. Practically all of them go to the United States, where universities are much better than in China, and diplomas from U.S. universities are the most highly prized on the Chinese market. Many of these students remain in the United States after graduation, because they enjoy both high earnings and much greater personal, academic, and ideological freedom. Besides, returning to a Chinese university seems difficult for anyone who does not have a solid network of family relations. Out of a million young Chinese who went abroad between 1978 and 2006, only 275,000 returned.[38] My sense is that the majority of academics who have so far responded to appeals from the Beijing authorities to return are at the end of their careers or have been called back by their families, and that in contrast the United States' attractiveness is growing among those who have in principle chosen a "Chinese" career—which is not without some advantages for Beijing. The conclusion is clear: China will keep its elites or induce them to return only when it offers adequate financial resources and political space. Until then the harsh judgment of Guy Sorman will remain valid: "China has not created a brand, innovation, or manufacturing process of world standard."[39]

Entry Tickets to the World

A final category of costs arise from China's entry into the world. For a certain period of time, the country managed the extraordinary feat of taking its first steps in the world without paying the slightest price. Its Western partners agreed in thinking that it was coming from a long way off; for the sake of peace, it was worth inviting it to the table for free. For its part, the Chinese leadership willingly accepted this graciousness, which saved it money and spared it from internal debate; it could always withdraw later. Willingly or not, the clever Westerners set up large cooperative programs, which increased the attractiveness of the larger world to the Chinese. The Chinese soon understood that there was a good deal to be gained from more thorough commercial involvement. But then they had to pay up. So they pleaded their underdevelopment and then emphasized their membership in the vague category of "Third World countries" to obtain reductions. But these were only temporary expedients: to achieve real status, China finally had to contribute in every possible way to the world as it is. It paid its dues to multilateral organizations, multiplied its number of missions, paid its diplomats better, increased fellowships for professors and students, participated in various humanitarian operations, and fulfilled an increasing portion of its international commitments. Against expectations, it even respected fairly well the free trade agreements it had made to join the WTO—and it is true that it derived even greater benefits from having made them. And it finally discovered the delights—and expenses—of soft power by increasing the number of Confucius Institutes worldwide, intended to spread Chinese language and culture.

Another example of an entry ticket into the world is the increase in the value of the yuan, which is insistently called for by American and European authorities, because its undervaluing inequitably favors Chinese exports. In principle, the Beijing authorities are not hostile to this step, but they demand that the adjustment be gradual; for example, they have to avoid provoking the collapse of Chinese grain producers in the face of Canadian and Australian imports. And indeed, the value of the Chinese currency in relation to the dollar has increased by almost 20 percent since 2003. There are two reasons for that: to drive the Chinese economy's move into high-end production and—this is a new argument—to respond to pressure the Chinese authorities feel from their Western partners. Yet another price to be paid by a country that long has enjoyed a free ride.

What Will Happen to the Chinese Growth Rate?

It is difficult not to think that all these new costs will have an effect on the rate of growth. I surveyed recognized experts on the Chinese economy on the question. In some cases, either pessimism or optimism was extreme. In the pessimistic camp is Diana Hochraich, one of the few experts to anticipate the Asian financial crisis of 1997–1998. She thinks the Chinese economy is advancing too rapidly, suffers from fundamental deficiencies, and will long remain in a dependent relationship to the vital centers of globalization.[40] In the optimistic camp, the members of the French Economic Mission in Beijing skillfully explained to me that production and social insurance costs borne by the Chinese economy were only one of the variables affecting Chinese economic growth. They pointed to future progress in labor efficiency and judged that in case of difficulties, China could use the huge amount of funds in its foreign reserves.

A majority of other experts, while considering that the Chinese economy should reduce its growth rate as much as possible, remained moderately optimistic; either they thought, like Françoise Lemoine, that it could stabilize growth at around 7 percent, or, like Daniel Haber, that it would resume its forward march after the temporary difficulties following the 2008 Olympics or the Universal Exposition in Shanghai in 2010. Haber pointed to two positive factors that have not yet shown their importance: the formation of a domestic consumer market and the internationalization of large Chinese companies. And in a book published in 2006, François Gipouloux predicts an annual growth rate between 5 and 7 percent up to 2010.[41]

In 2006, the Chinese authorities themselves were counting on a growth rate of 7.5 percent up to the same date, and in late 2007 they anticipated 8 percent growth for 2008. Most consulting firms remain relatively optimistic, but it should be noted that in early September 2007, Standard and Poor's justified its relative pessimism by the slowdown in the American economy. In January 2008, Goldman Sachs was still anticipating 10 percent growth for the year in progress, arguing that increased domestic demand would compensate to some degree for the American recession.[42] But as information about the slowdown in the United States and Europe accumulated, forecasts were lowered: Barclays, for example, estimated 8.8 percent, the World Bank 9.6 percent. There was even a Harvard economics professor who predicted a "recession," meaning growth below 6 percent.[43] Of course, as one expert said to me with a smile, "economists are especially skilled at predicting the past." Nonetheless, there are situations in economics, as elsewhere, in which reason can risk expressing doubt and lay out divergent hypotheses.

I believe that is the case today. Although I am not a specialist, a corrective shift downward in Chinese growth seems to me inevitable. Accidents are often mentioned: an American crisis that would suddenly reduce outlets for Chinese exports, a stock market disturbance facilitated by the overheated state of Chinese exchanges that would spread to the banking system, or a new inflationary impulse that the spike in food prices and an average price hike of 6 percent have led analysts to fear since the fall of 2007.[44] These hypothetical outcomes are unpredictable, but they help justify the authorities' policy of reducing the rate of growth. In any event, it seems to me undoubtedly true that the Chinese economy will be unable to maintain its rate of growth for two primary reasons: the first is that its costs are in any circumstance going to increase rapidly, and the second is that the authorities themselves are pursuing a resolute policy, which they are probably going to have to tighten, and that should at least have a slowing effect.

In addition, several factors could contribute to hastening the slow-down. For example, it is quite possible that after the 2008 Olympics and the Universal Exposition in Shanghai in 2010, the Chinese economy will experience a kind of countermovement, attributable, for example, to the decline in construction projects and other major public projects. More-over, some international factors could intensify the slowdown: foreign markets could lose vitality and openness, as the increasing difficulties in trade relations with the United States lead one to fear; besides, at a time when it will have to invest to enter high-technology production sectors, China will face new competition (for example, from Vietnam and India) in labor-intensive industries.

Failure Is Not Foreordained

For all of that, it is practically just as difficult for me to trust the predic-tions of disaster that began to be heard in the middle of 2007. I dislike the almost automatic way in which former Maoists who have become hos-tile to the Beijing regime blithely transfer onto the economy the hopes for catastrophe that the Chinese political system has not realized. And I think we have to listen to the arguments of diplomats and businessmen who think that China is still a good bet. In their view, a movement of eco-nomic emancipation this powerful does not collapse all at once, and a momentary crisis would not necessarily be catastrophic. The effect that a shock of the same magnitude as that suffered by the American economy between 1929 and 1933 would have on the Chinese economy has been calculated: a decline of 27 percent in the Chinese GDP, which would set it back only three years.[45] The Chinese leaders will have the means to react in the face of the anticipated difficulties: foreign exchange reserves, fiscal and budgetary margins, rural labor reserves, significant room for increasing labor efficiency. And this is why the Chinese economy has reasonable chances of stabilizing its growth at a more than acceptable level.

More broadly, it could be said that China has entered a new cycle. For the first time in a long time, failure is no longer inevitable for the country. Until the late 1990s, I was more pessimistic, as were a number of other observers. While recognizing the magnitude of the changes introduced by the policies of Deng Xiaoping, I doubted that the international and domestic circumstances would enable China to escape from the decline that had begun under the empire and that the communist disaster had in fact confirmed. I did not imagine that America would want to—and be able to—exhaust Chinese communism in the way that it had its Soviet counterpart. From this perspective, the alignment with the United States against Moscow decided on by Mao Zedong in the late 1960s was a saving stroke of genius. And I doubted that Chinese society, exhausted by decades of violence and crushed by campaigns of totalitarian repression, would find within itself the strength necessary for its emancipation.

What I did not understand soon enough was that, pressed by the triumph of a globalized capitalism, the Chinese regime had itself decided on change. It doesn't matter whether or not Deng Xiaoping understood in advance which way he was going. The fact is that in the international circumstances of the time his strategy of giving priority to growth carried two fortunate angles of approach. One shifted the Chinese economic model toward a kind of managed mercantilism. The other simply returned China to the world. The last decisions Deng Xiaoping made in 1992 and the interpretation of them in the following years by the team of Jiang Zemin and Zhu Rongji consisted of accepting these two approaches. Whatever its concern to set itself apart, the new team of Hu

Jintao and Wen Jiabao, though innovative, continues that strategy. Its program encourages optimism because, as I have shown, it has two necessary goals: the construction of a state able to take control of the special interest mafias and a more fully mastered and more qualitative involvement in the global world of today.

The country is thus guided by a rational project, one adapted to the economic circumstances, and it is linked to the ambitions that Chinese reformers have held since the late nineteenth century. In addition, although doubts weigh on the immediate future, the international economic circumstances are still favorable overall: no military threat on the borders, growing diplomatic influence, and easy access to all markets and supplies of raw materials. Abroad as domestically, China is in a more favored situation than at any time over the last two centuries. So much the better, because the coming test could be harsh.

Chapter 5

The Acceleration of History

The Acid Test for the Government

THE PROSPECT, THEN, IS FOR A REDUCTION IN THE RATE OF
growth, or stagnation, perhaps worse. This will be an acid test for the
government, the seriousness of which will depend on its magnitude.

The first reason for this is that the new difficulties will force the political apparatus and its clients to restrain the appetites that they have
steadily developed—and satisfied—over the last three decades. The sacrifices will no doubt fall more heavily on the people, but they will also
affect entrepreneurs, who will be forced to reduce their profits, and
more widely the tens of millions of government officials. Under Mao
Zedong, their living conditions were generally Spartan—what made
the job particularly difficult was the demanding, suspicious, and unpredictable central authority. Subsequently, under Deng Xiaoping, officials

enjoyed a real bonanza. While traditional command careers remained, new opportunities arose to "dive into the sea" of business. As Jean-Louis Rocca has shown, for CCP officials, the period was one of professional and social "overlapping."[1] Nothing was excluded. Because corruption was both necessary and universal, the only danger for the manager of a company was that his enemies might be powerful enough to compromise him in a corruption scandal. In exchange, the requirements for these new positions were generally limited: managers could make up for their professional limitations or even incompetence through their political connections and their supporters in the banking system. For example, the directors of state-owned factories or more or less privatized companies had successful careers greased by bank loans that soon became bad debts.

It is clear that this little world will have to live less lavishly and under the supervision of the central government. Indeed, to remedy its bad reputation, the government will be forced to make itself into the guardian of law and morality, for example, by more extensively using the neo-Confucian vocabulary that it has already updated. Rivalries between victims of moral censure might come to light. New tensions will appear between technical and political and central and regional officials, as well as between some of them and entrepreneurs. The unity of the plutobureaucratic class that now dominates China will be seriously tested.

In the second place, economic difficulties will severely test the ability of the government, particularly its leadership, to react. We will then see whether, like Zhu Rongji in 1998, it will be able to find the right solution, for the field of experts has grown, but their divergences have also flourished; business circles also have government connections; and foreign partners are no longer wary of offering advice and warnings. We will see especially whether the government can impose its solution on an apparatus that is heavily influenced by regional and local interests and can make the law of Beijing rule over all of the microclimates.

A major question will no doubt be whether the government reacts like a party or like a state. In the first case, it will rely largely on propaganda and police and will be in danger of securing obedience more apparent than real. In the other case, economic difficulties could provide an important opportunity for the state in China to progress, and with it the notions of public good and public function, in which case the application of official policies could gain increased effectiveness.

Will the People Have to Suffer Without Hope?

For its part, the population, which bore up under the government's work discipline[2] only in exchange for a swift improvement in its standard of living, will have to get used to much lower rates of growth. As a result, depending on the magnitude of the new sacrifices, the implicit but very solid contract between government and society that shored up Chinese political stability will be more or less clearly challenged.

Movements of discontent are likely to be magnified by the memory of the people's suffering under communism. This memory will one day be restored: people know of the constantly repeated promises no less constantly translated into terror by Maoist power, and then, after a form of liberation, of disappointments and unpleasant surprises under Deng Xiaoping, and now of the hardships of a far from harmonious society. By the mid-1980s, peasant income had stopped growing significantly. Over the next decade, city dwellers suffered from unemployment and the disappearance of the "iron rice bowl" of the *danwei* (work units). At the same time, both peasants and urbanites had to assume their own new health and education costs. In the end, life was better but more difficult than before.

At least suffering was assuaged by a continuous rise in living standards, and even more by that rise's predictability. The majority of the Chinese are poor, and almost all of them live as though they were poor. They watch what they consume while hoping for quick income increases that would enable them either to pay off their debts or to save, because they are aware of the heavy expenses awaiting every Chinese household: education and marriage costs for the children, the purchase of a home and medical expenses for the old.

Growth is therefore the basic ingredient for a society that lives in order to save and has very few resources to consume. It also fosters the hope of the poor for a better future: if not for themselves, at least for their children. Peasants think of establishing their children in a city, and city dwellers save money to send them to the best universities. The regular and rapid rise in income compensates for the difficulties and uncertainties that the commodification of the economy has introduced into daily life. A decline in growth would cause surprise and anxiety.

The Chinese would enter the world of low growth numbers, where the old countries of the West are currently becalmed, but the Chinese will enter it under entirely different circumstances: first, admittedly, because they will not approach, or not immediately, the near stagnation that we Westerners are experiencing. But we came to this situation when we were not only developed but had entered the consumer society; the Chinese, in contrast, are not completely developed, and most of them still only dream of the consumer society. They have too great a need to hope to accept a situation in which the possibility of providing for the future would be severely limited.

The End of the Contract Between the Regime and the Population?

That is not all. Economic growth has a very powerful meaning in China in the aftermath of its tragic experiences. It is both proof that the regime has changed, because it is doing something for the population, and it is an essential clause of the implicit contract that ties it to the population and underlies the order of things. To understand how necessary this guarantee is, one has to understand how deeply ordinary citizens despise their masters.

This phenomenon is often ignored or neglected, because no large-scale rebellion ever raised the Chinese people against communism: as in the Soviet Union, the system's shackles were too powerful to permit a clear view of what a revolt would lead to. But, starting from the first "great wave of socialism" in 1955, opposition and popular disaffection have appeared almost continuously and in every possible way: escapism, passivity, sabotage, fakery, and so on. These reactions subsided only in the rare periods when some temporary concessions were granted, and then everyone had to take advantage of them as quickly as possible because no one had any illusions that they would last.

When Deng Xiaoping came to power, things changed both a good deal and very little. With a lucidity that seems remarkable in retrospect, the urban and, even more, the rural population played the game the new government was proposing. They went back to work, often taking their meager savings out of hiding to invest in small private enterprises, which were gradually becoming lawful, like the garage mechanic I met in 1984 in the hills of southern Zhejiang south of Shanghai, who had begun by setting up a bicycle repair stand at his doorstep and gradually started repairing and then selling scooters, motorcycles, and finally automobiles. The Chinese people believed in Deng Xiaoping's promises— that made all the difference with Gorbachev's USSR—and they were right to do so. Proof came very quickly, by the early 1980s, when the dismantling of the people's communes, the authorization of family farming, and then of the private sale of a growing number of agricultural products made possible a spectacular increase in peasant income.

But the opportunism with which the population profited from the reforms never turned into political allegiance. Everyone had soon noticed that the leaders had not changed: if they weren't always the same men, they were at least the same type of men, who merely had a little more hesitation than before in resorting to violence. The propaganda had scarcely changed, and it presented as concessions, gifts, and finally means to power what for the people was the essential: an improvement in living standards. The only unquestionable change in their eyes was for the worse, and that was corruption. Hence ordinary people developed a combination of feelings of opportunism, indifference, and contempt toward the people at the top.

Opportunism was certainly much more intense than under Mao, because it was a time when success or failure could be determined at every moment. But profiting from the game did not prevent indifference toward one's masters. Under Mao, this indifference had been latent, but political pressure forced people to be vigilant. But once its survival was guaranteed and hope had entered its life—a hope with little political coloration and far from communist ideals—the population became indifferent to politics. It paid as little attention as possible, even at high points. The annual session of the Chinese National Assembly and Senate caused traffic jams that people sniggered at, and television programs on party congresses aroused nothing but indifference. The depoliticization of Chinese society has reached peaks seldom matched anywhere in the world.

During my time in China, I sometimes pointed out to my interlocutors that, compared to their predecessors, their leaders were not so bad, because they were making very rapid progress and were also concerned with the life of the people. I was often answered with an avalanche of bitter remarks that said in substance: how can we trust the social intentions of a corrupt regime that reserves important advantages for its own people? How can we be sure that it will not soon make new mistakes?

Things are clear at this point. Growth is simply indispensable to create popular obedience, it is the regime's only legitimacy, and it has to be rapid because no one has confidence in the future. This is how the regime's stability is organized, and it also explains the danger hovering over it.

The End of the "Pigeons"

Where could this danger arise? One critical sector is that of the Western markets, where Chinese exporters make their highest profits. The American market is the principal one. This market is financially and psychologically essential to present-day China, yet it is also one of those over which China has the most limited control, for, after all, low Chinese prices are no guarantee of consumer taste and even less of the health of the American economy. If an accident were to occur, it seems clear that Beijing could do little about it. And the danger is getting closer. The American economy began slowing in the summer of 2007.[3] In addition, various export scandals (particularly involving toys) tarnished the image of China in the United States (in Japan as well), while human rights associations continued their campaign against the Beijing Olympics.

Europe was also the scene of numerous recurring disputes on Chinese trade practices and the excesses of repression in the country. In the same French lycées where geography teachers had applauded Chinese people's communes forty years before, the legitimate language became—to excess—the condemnation of China for its contempt for human rights.

Of course, Western opinion has not turned completely hostile, especially because business circles are counting on Chinese growth. But it is not impossible that the question of foreign investment will soon be opened up. It is still protected by a kind of "holy alliance" that has agreed to conceal often very unpleasant facts with an effectiveness confirmed by the continuous growth of foreign direct investment in China: $74 billion in 2007, making a cumulative total of about $760 billion.[4] In fact, only a minority of projects are prepared and carried out with the necessary precautions, resources, and follow-up. With only slight exaggeration, it can be said that the "holy alliance" is basically made up of foreign investors who are fleeced and the Chinese economic circles that fleece them. It is held together by the fact that some of them find a primarily psychological benefit in investing—castles in the air and romantic illusions, publicity, the high life—and others a concrete advantage in getting technology in return for selling their land and labor force. Its security is guaranteed by the fact that the governments of the former derive a propaganda advantage from it, and the Chinese government gets concrete benefits substantial enough to sell a policy of opening to the world that was at first challenged.

It would be good to have impartial investigations of the number and identity of the Western firms—for Taiwanese, Japanese, and Singaporean companies seem to have better success—whose investments have turned out to be profitable or who have at least recovered their investment. On this point, there are only rumors or fragmentary and unreliable surveys. But I have not forgotten what an excellent economic correspondent confided in me on the eve of his departure from Beijing: only one-fourth of French investors had so far recovered the amount of their original investment.[5]

There are increasing reasons for thinking that light will finally be shed on the subject, first because investing in China is going to become even less profitable. To attract investors, China had to promise them advantages of all sorts that it is beginning to rescind: for example, it restored taxes on foreign companies to the norm (25 instead of 15 percent)—taxes that the companies are compelled to pay, unlike many of their Chinese competitors, just as they can no longer avoid applying social legislation. In addition, Chinese costs are constantly growing, so that India has become an increasingly attractive destination. Although it has inferior public services, India is much less expensive, particularly when it comes to labor, and that is becoming ever more widely known. It is therefore beginning to overcome the huge gap in foreign investments, and many observers think that in short order it will be competing vigorously with China for investments in "workshop" industries. This forecast was confirmed in the fall of 2007 by an UNCTAD survey and by a report from Capgemini covering 340 world-class companies.[6]

Second, apparently starting a short time ago, Chinese firms have been using and even manipulating the opening of their country in a questionable way. With the complicity of the authorities, including the judiciary, and a heavy dash of impudence, some of them have been plundering their Western partners. For example, Schneider Electric was found guilty of "counterfeiting" and required to pay its Chinese competitor €31 million. One of its directors provides a striking summary of the affair: "When they sued us, they could prove that we were using that technology, because it was ours before it was theirs." And the Danone-Wahaha affair that came to light in 2007 showed in succession the predatory maneuvers of a Chinese firm bought by Danone that had resumed autonomous activity by marketing heavily imitative products; the distracted naïveté long displayed by the French firm when faced with these operations, followed by a ballet of boastful declarations; and unconscionable negotiations conducted by the Chinese firm that relied on a law intended to protect the economic independence of the country. I do not know what happened next in this distressing melodrama. Nor, in the absence of open sources, do I have the means to assess the representative character of these episodes. But there is no great risk in foreseeing a more or less sharp reduction in foreign investments.

Third is the problem of energy. China is at the mercy of supplies that are difficult to protect and whose prices are outside its control. What is to be done? After long neglecting the question, Chinese leaders have been dealing with it since 2004 in a way that has been both frenzied and disorganized. Unable to establish an effective foothold in the Middle Eastern theater, they have shown interest in Russian gas and Central Asian oil deposits, with mixed results. The penetration of Africa has been more successful, and that continent now supplies about 20 percent of the oil China consumes.[7] But this policy is costly from every point of view. Not only have Chinese importers caused prices to rise, but their large-scale maneuvers have stirred up anxiety in some countries and major diplomatic difficulties in others: for example, Beijing provoked a worldwide scandal by protecting the bloody dictatorship in Sudan before eventually attempting to extract concessions from it; in Zimbabwe, on the other hand, after some spectacular disappointments, Chinese diplomacy has had to resign itself to waiting for the successor to the despot Robert Mugabe. An analogous problem has arisen in a bordering Asian country, Burma, where the repression of popular protest by a predatory junta has endangered the reputation of Chinese diplomacy, at first concerned with protecting supplies of wood and precious stones but now becoming increasingly aware of the diplomatic price of its attitude.

The fourth critical sector consists of both the large Chinese banks and their client companies in interior China, the majority of which are state-connected companies under great financial difficulties but that the provincial authorities consider indispensable to maintain employment. The banks lend, the companies waste, and "defeasance" companies established by the state buy up the bad debts: this is the pathway that keeps the system simultaneously in danger and alive. But it is impossible not to fear that in case of difficulties the banks will reduce their subsidies. Then they will be attacked by their clients, and bankruptcies will mushroom, bringing down larger segments of the economy.

The last crucial sector is the stock markets of Shanghai and Shenzhen. The hundred million amateur market players brought in by the inflation of the summer of 2007 are both a resource for and a weakness of the stock market system. The great majority of them have no training and are swayed by the wildest rumors—there have already been violent downturns provoked by mere hearsay about potential government measures. Panics are probable, and they would likely magnify difficulties and weaken the major economic groups that are the spearhead of the Chinese economy. Market players' anxiety would then be likely to turn into anger against the authorities that promoted stock market activity and would therefore be considered responsible for the new course of things.[8]

Indiscipline and Proclivity for the Extremes

As I have said, the Chinese authorities have the means to react. But they cannot afford to make a mistake, because two characteristics of Chinese society are likely to accentuate the difficulties.

The first defect is the indiscipline that prevails in China. It is hard to assess from abroad, because the images of Maoist China are still present to our minds. Admirably transmitted or interpreted by successful authors such as Alain Peyrefitte and intelligently used by the Beijing authorities, these images have given rise to a radical misunderstanding: in fact, China was not disciplined by nature but temporarily terrorized.

Under Mao, popular indiscipline came to the surface only when police pressure relaxed. It has intensified over the last three decades because of the easing of constraints, the improvement of living standards, and an expansion of the private sphere, all of which give individuals the desire and the means to defend their own interests. The examples of this indiscipline are legion: for example, birth control was never completely applied in the countryside, and in cities only a minority of households concerned filed a tax return in 2007—besides, the authorities would have a great deal of difficulty finding out where the many violators live.

To be sure, this indiscipline is not very politicized. There are few individuals who do not have serious reasons to criticize the various levels of government, but even fewer who are looking for a confrontation. But indiscipline governs everyday activities. Automobile traffic in Beijing is an extraordinary example. Speeding and running red lights are rare, but the population as a whole, including the police, pays no attention to the other main principles of the rules of the road: right of way, signaling, parking. But this indiscipline is not entirely lawless. It adheres to a few principles, just as the indiscipline of rural communities with respect to birth control obeys customary principles that favor large families and male children. In cities, the three principles of indiscipline on the road are priority to the largest vehicles, to those already engaged in a maneuver, and to cars driven by residents of the area.

Insofar as it often characterizes majority behavior, Chinese-style indiscipline gives way only before its absolute opposite: a police raid or a mass campaign. By stifling originally moderate measures, such campaigns inspire in the authorities excesses of authoritarianism. This is a partial explanation for the mobilizations Mao Zedong relied on to make an indifferent population obey him. From them flowed the seesawing character of Chinese social and political life: every exaggeration had to be rectified and compensated for by "consolidations" that were so many partial retreats. When there is no question of offering material compensation to people who apply the law, there is no alternative but to exaggerate its provisions and the associated penalties. It is reasonable to think that the general passivity that since 2004 has greeted government appeals to reduce the rate of growth will give way only to harsher measures.

Current Chinese leaders are both lucid and cautious. Because they suffered directly from it during the Cultural Revolution, they distrust the proclivity for extremes so characteristic of Chinese society. They know it could transform simple economic difficulties into a crisis. But they might forgo this caution if economic difficulties became epidemic: stock market panic, banking crises, factory closings. They could then be forced to change direction radically, which would provoke a scarcely less dangerous situation of demoralization and a general sense of "every man for himself."

It is therefore reasonable to doubt China's ability to overcome critical situations without worsening them. From this perspective, the experience with SARS was significant. The government was able to treat the problem—which specialists realized at the beginning was serious but limited—only by exaggerating it and by using totalitarian methods of control, including closing workplaces and confining individuals at home. The situation was well summed up by a Chinese businessman: "In a one-party country everything looks peaceful, but when there's a problem, it's a big problem."[9]

The Return of Politics

For all these reasons, there is a likelihood of significant popular unrest, particularly in places closest to the government and the most visible to Chinese and Western journalists. Anything is possible: incidents in front of banks, looting of large stores, mobs in front of public buildings—all incidents that have already happened in isolated instances: for example, the Zhongguancun Wal-Mart in Beijing was wrecked in January 2005 by migrant workers furious at not having been paid. It is easy to imagine that new employment problems would provide a mass of the unemployed for such disturbances, for it is too often forgotten that present-day China has millions of unemployed workers—official statistics are not reliable, but the figure of 11 percent is most often mentioned.[10] Among the unemployed are many former workers in state-owned factories who have maintained habits of solidarity. But the most active might be young university graduates, ever larger numbers of whom are waiting for a job—only 50 percent of them found a place upon graduation in 2005.[11] Considering the nature and seriousness of the stakes as well as the high likelihood of police missteps, popular protest would probably be violent. Even more than in 1989, an important issue in the crisis would be the attitude of the media, which have developed considerably in the interim and which have many young journalists who finally want to do their job correctly. New means of communication, particularly mobile phones, would facilitate both the organization of disturbances and the journalists' access to information. But the authorities could just as well use them to spread false news or communicate prohibitions.

Some observers consider it possible there will be an increase in power of a democratic opposition, the only group able, in their view, of holding the communist elites accountable for their mistakes and opening up a political future. This hypothesis seems to me illusory. The democratic option has been compromised in present-day China as much through its recent failures and the spectacle presented by Western democracies as by the recent successes of the regime. Only a few courageous groups remain, a few writers known abroad, or real witnesses, such as, recently, Hu Jia, a defender of AIDS victims who was indicted for "subversion" for bringing to light Beijing's failure to meet the commitments it had made before the Olympic Games. Moreover, the government is still powerful enough to crush any eventual democratic movement.

Indeed, the slogans that currently seem the most popular and that have turned up in many recent incidents are those that denounce "injustice," "inequality," the corruption of the rich and powerful, or police excesses. Substantial masses of people could be mobilized around such slogans. Democratic activists might also slip into demonstrations, as could others from religious sects. But some CCP leaders could just as easily take hold of this populist vocabulary and divert it to support a kind of Chinese "Bonapartism."

It is hard to imagine, in the early stages at least, that the police would not manage to protect the official order, at least as long as the government remains united. The key to events, as in 1989, would be the degree of the CCP's internal cohesion—it will be remembered that the events of the spring had been authorized by the split that had occurred at the highest level. And the cohesion of the CCP has already been undermined by the erosion of the ideological credo, the divergence between local and bureaucratic interests, and often by competition between career and business interests. At present, although the formation of factions is banned—and is futile as long as the regime is successful—the CCP harbors almost all the political sensibilities a Westerner can imagine: liberals, republicans, social democrats, populists, and finally conservative or reformist communists, real or apparent.

All these splits remain discreet because of political control and even more because of the lack of political opportunities: when the rate of growth reaches 10 percent, reasons for divisiveness decline. The splits that appear in public are the least unacceptable to the government. The conflict between advocates of reform and supporters of the dogma was of considerable importance in the 1980s,[12] but it subsequently lost a good deal of its importance after the death of most of the old guard. The reformists were crushed, and the conservatives are just getting by—or have succumbed to the siren's song of money.

This split apparently dissolved during the 1990s into a division that is much more commonplace in other latitudes. This is a division between supporters of social justice, who claim to be on "the left," and supporters of economic liberalism, that is, permissiveness toward companies. Political liberalism has not fared well, although it has not disappeared: Tocqueville still is an influence in universities. The balance between these two poles has slightly shifted in the last twenty years. Up to a certain point, Jiang Zemin's team tended to favor a lax attitude toward business, whereas Hu Jintao and Wen Jiabao have adopted more populist positions that pass for encouragements to the left.

Another commonplace division is that between the advocates and opponents of an opening to the nationalists of every variety who have proliferated since the mid-1980s. This is an odd split, because it internally divides a large number of intellectuals and leaders. Many of them are advocates of an opening of the country and for a greater role of China in the world, favored the organization of the Olympic Games and the victories of Chinese teams, support foreign investors and the reduction of their privileges, and support economic cooperation with Taiwan and retaking the dissident island by force if necessary. This is a reason for the volatile and changing character of Chinese policies in areas where nationalism is most at issue: with respect to Vietnam, Japan, and North Korea, for example, diplomatic shifts have been numerous. These fluctuations have become customary to the extent that there are frequent rumors of an offensive against Taiwan, whereas in reality relations with the island have unquestionably improved.

The current line of the Chinese leadership straddles these various splits intelligently: it is less hostile than its predecessor to a conservative core that no longer represents a real danger, but in words it has also shown itself to be less antidemocratic for the same reason; however, it has offered substantial satisfaction to the nationalist movement and the "left." In fact, it is primarily focused on reducing peripheral discontents so as to be able to concentrate on the essential: achieving better control over the central government and the provincial authorities in order to direct economic policy more effectively.

One may try to imagine how, bereft of the success that ensured its cohesion and shaken by significant social disturbances in the sight of the entire world, the Chinese Communist Party could split along political or even factional lines, and also according to possibly contradictory regional or provincial lines: for example, the coastal provinces all share an interest in openness, but some of them are burdened by the power of Shanghai or Guangzhou.

If economic difficulties turned out to be limited or of short duration, these internal divisions would be rather quickly absorbed to permit the more or less complete suppression of social movements. But if the crisis was serious and lasting, one may imagine that these divisions could deepen. Factional groupings or even embryonic parties would find it advantageous to organize elections to count their numbers.

Let's go further. From those elections, if they were relatively free, would come more or less pluralist assemblies at national and provincial levels, which would demand to control government bodies. A process of democratization would get under way, not arising from a social revolution or a democratic movement but because of the breakup of the ruling party. Once condemned for its failure in 1989, democracy would be reborn from the division of its conquerors, in a sense by default, and its advocates, defeated and at first a minority, could return to the stage for a time.

A Very Strange Democratization

Let's be frank: it is not certain that a democratic process would go as far as elections, and it is even less certain that it would take on the ideal colors that democratic activists, in China and abroad, hope for. It is hard to see how disorder, or even chaos, the *luan* that haunts the history of China, could be avoided—a disorder in proportion to the magnitude of the economic difficulties and social disturbances.

Like governments that have succeeded one another over the centuries, the communist regime has long wielded and is still brandishing the threat of disorder to justify its domination. But in fact, through the accumulation of its excesses and its past mistakes as well as the limited changes of the recent period, it has made disorder almost inevitable. First, it disqualified politics by its totalitarian practice, and then by its exclusive concentration on economic performance. Then it accustomed the population to the use of violence both through its own crimes and by unleashing the power of money, and it is now promising a legalization that it is quite incapable of applying completely. It has therefore created a social body that is suffering from violence but that easily turns to it, that passionately desires order but that eludes it whenever possible, that dreams of a more just future but that does not believe in it—and that carefully refrains from risking anything to hasten its advent.

How far would the disorder spread? If the difficulties turn out to be temporary and if no major crisis affects the country's international environment, the worst should be avoided. The country is in fact not without resources, and the rest of the world would not be able to abandon it. In any event, it would pay close attention to events in the coastal regions of China that contain most of the country's economic potential and where the major foreign presence is found. Hence, significant areas of China would remain more or less sheltered.

But some geopolitical disorder would at least begin to come to the surface. A prediction that the country would fragment would be an exaggeration: over time, despite everything, the dream of Chinese unity has finally acquired some reality, particularly because the central government is a very significant political and financial resource. What seems more likely is, to a variable degree depending on circumstances, an intensification of interprovincial conflict over impoverishment, a sort of universal "every man for himself" in slow motion, in which the coastal provinces would inevitably mark their superiority over their poorer neighbors with fewer contacts in the West. Added to the divergences in development between provinces would be variations in their subordination to the central government. These phenomena would interfere with the circulation of goods from and to the interior, thereby increasing the existing advantages of the favored coastal regions.

These hypotheses are fragile, but they have the virtue of evoking the fate of the former Soviet Union. The two countries, it will be recalled, had a series of similarities: a huge territory, no borders with a major democracy (India is really far from China proper), a communist history, no long and decisive democratic experience in the past, a still weak middle class, NGOs with insufficient power, political personnel trained in authoritarian procedures and a population accustomed to strong central authority, and leaders accustomed to mixing business with politics. In the USSR, it was the Communist Party itself that split and lost most of its substance, and democracy came directly out of this political and regional decomposition. This did not prevent its subsequent manipulation in support of nationalist and mafia-like authoritarianism.

A similar pattern might occur in China: rising disorder would bring about a call for authoritarian government while limiting its effectiveness. The government would rely on large financial groups and to govern would turn to the nationalist verbiage that the communist regime has steadily encouraged over the past two decades.

We should not conclude that this would lead to a return to some sort of totalitarian system. The disfavor of communism, the opening up of the country, the experience of individual freedom, and the passion for money should bar the restoration of harsh social discipline. Too many new habits and disorders have taken root since the death of Mao. In China as elsewhere, a totalitarian regime is an experience of limits that will not be repeated. But in China as in the former Soviet Union, totalitarianism has more easily given way to various forms of authoritarianism than to its democratic opposite.[13]

For example, whether or not still under the name of the Communist Party, there could be a kind of Guomindang—the old nationalist party founded by Sun Yat-sen that Chiang Kai-shek had led to power and then defeat at the hands of the communists in 1949: a remodeled Guomindang, with an ideological façade with a social, Confucian, and technocratic vocabulary; vaguely representative institutions perhaps with property qualifications; a more discreet system of social control; and an officially all-powerful leadership, but one that would allow factions and financial and local interests to operate. A regime of this kind would probably take some care to maintain an appearance of democratic conformity and even more care of various commercial and financial interests. But like the Guomindang, it would make nationalism its basic program, both domestically to deal with centrifugal tendencies and calm social discontent and internationally to compensate for the loss of influence engendered by economic difficulties and in response to the rise of major Asian neighbors such as Japan, Korea, and India.

This is a future that is simultaneously more dangerous and more complicated than had been anticipated, but it is also one that is more open.

Book III

The Great Riddles of the Future

WHEN I DISCUSSED THE FUTURE OF THEIR COUNTRY WITH Chinese friends, they quickly summarized their doubts and then concentrated on the major problems they had to resolve if the country were to mature, and on this subject they were inexhaustible. I think the way they are thinking about the issue is correct: it is easier to determine what the future of China will depend on than to figure out what it will be.

Chapter 6

Can China Be Governed?

The Folly of Unity

THE FACT IS SO WIDELY KNOWN THAT FEW MAKE THE EFFORT to think about it: China is not only immense (3.7 million square miles), but it is also the most populated country in the world, accounting for about 20 percent of the world's population. The fact that India is on the way to catching up with the Chinese population does not justify playing down the problem, because India at least is an explicitly federal state, like Canada, Brazil, and Russia, nations the sociologist Ignacy Sachs calls "whales in the global ocean." China shares with them the huge burdens of space or demography or both. But it is the only one that claims to be unitary, thereby depriving itself of the means to establish an administration adapted to its internal diversity, for example, a federal or confederal regime.

The claim to unity is ritually admired by many Westerners and is for many Chinese a motive for self-admiration that ought not to deceive lucid observers. Indeed, the arguments marshaled to support China's claim to exceptional status are questionable. The first one is historical: the supposed millennia of unitary history. But those millennia began just before the Christian era, in a much smaller space than the country's current territory, and they were interrupted by sometimes lengthy periods of division. Besides, the empire tolerated all sorts of situations within its borders. Again in the recent past, from 1916 to 1927 and from 1937 to 1949, China was de facto divided into several entities. The second argument is linguistic. The written language is indeed a very powerful shared characteristic, but there are many examples worldwide of groups of states that share a single language. Moreover, "standard" Chinese, the dialect of Beijing, is spoken by only half the population, despite a theoretically uniform system of education.

The cultural argument is only slightly stronger, because Chinese culture has not yet completely conquered the non-native zones of the territory—almost 50 percent—occupied by ethnic minorities that have been weakened but are often restive. Thus "China" is not completely at home everywhere in China itself. For although it is true that Chinese economic influence is spreading everywhere and that the Beijing government is no longer facing any major obstacles, it is nonetheless true that its cultural attraction has encountered considerable barriers locally. When you go, for example, to "Little Tibet," in Gansu, in the northwest of the country, you notice both that no national minority there is in a condition to offer serious resistance to political control and economic penetration by the Han ethnic group, the Tibetans least of all, and you also realize that the Muslim and Tibetan societies there are only partially Sinicized. Half of the Chinese territory is made up of ethnic, social, and cultural strata lacking in current political importance but whose future is unpredictable.

No doubt, the new political, military, and especially economic resources available to contemporary states have given Chinese unity more reality. In the eyes of history, one of the most important accomplishments of the communist regime will have been to have crushed in every possible way irredentist movements of Muslims, Mongols, and Tibetans. It also imposed on the entire country an extremely sturdy political, military, and police network. In a sense, that is the essential thing, because now it will take serious events to split the country.

But on the other hand, as time has passed, the political system has become largely cellular, and the economy has played an ambivalent role. The provinces enjoy extraordinary latitude for action, except in foreign policy, although most of them do carry on real economic diplomacy. The thirty provinces and major municipalities are all autonomous economic zones, each of which in its own way, depending on what is involved, can now thwart or retard the economic unity of the country and the policies of the center. To see this, all you need to do is order in one province a beer produced in the neighboring province.

Furthermore, within provinces, local identities of all magnitudes live side by side or compete or conflict, based on dialects often more widely spoken than standard Chinese, on rich and vital cultural repertories, and on identity reflexes that are so vigorous that CCP leaders have to endorse them. In the province of Henan, planted in the very center of the country, several alleged mausoleums of a hypothetical "first emperor," all superbly restored—not to say reconstructed—are intended to demonstrate that the Chinese imperial system was born there and not in the neighboring district.

Theoretically, the country is unitary, but in practice it is a more or less chaotic assemblage of fiefdoms that coexist and compete peacefully during periods of totalitarian constraint or prosperity but would find it intolerable to become impoverished together. Depending on the issues and the times, it operates like a federal state, a confederal state, or a congeries of isolated rural or urban villages. National laws, local regulations, and customary practices overlap and vary depending on the distance from the capital.[1] When the central government goes mad or fails, these circumstances provide shelters for the population. But those shelters can also hamper the application of better policies, as can be seen currently.

Overall, China is primarily unified by the upper levels of the CCP that dominates it, by the economic and social projects the party pursues, and by the enemies the party attributes to the country: in effect, by the political order, highway construction, and the hatred of Japan. Its unity is not absolutely without foundation, but it is incomplete and is also based on a number of circumstantial elements that a less authoritarian and more realistic politics would call into question or modify.

Unfortunately, this is a subject about which public discussion is prohibited, because the authorities realize that their position is fragile. It is to be hoped that one day a real debate will occur in China on the constitutional structure and identity of the country. The tragedy is that this path is currently blocked by Tibetan and Uighur demands, which Beijing exploits to prolong the status quo, and by the twofold obstacle of Taiwan: important elements of the Guomindang would condemn any federal steps, and those steps would be understood as an encouragement to Taiwanese dissidents. The result is a situation that fosters a spatially cellular arrangement. The regime ordinarily adapts to this, but it is an obstacle when the regime wants to reform.

Will the Provinces Obey?

The central authorities are aware of the obstacles that localisms place in front of their new policies, and they have been denouncing them with increasing force for the last several years—not without hypocrisy, for, after all, they have the power to appoint and dismiss important local officials. The most dangerous of these localisms is that of the richest provinces and municipalities, which had profited the most from the measures of decentralization adopted by Deng Xiaoping to launch the period of growth.[2] The center has somewhat trimmed the economic prerogatives of the provincial authorities by requiring authorizations for any new bank loans to go through Beijing. In a contrary direction, for a long time it has apparently not paid much attention to the proliferation of taxes theoretically intended to finance transportation and education, because it was encouraging local authorities to support themselves in those areas.[3] With regard to social policy, the center decided to applaud provincial and municipal officials who were active rather than to sanction the countless other localities that did nothing in this area. It seems that the highest authorities themselves bear substantial responsibility for the situation they are complaining about; this is corroborated by the fact that a majority of the Politburo of the CCP is made up of leaders who have served at the head of several provinces.

Several studies conducted a few years ago and published recently conclude that the power of the center over the provinces has been strengthened or at least maintained, highlighting the policy of oversight of officials, because it is centralized.[4] But these studies assess the application of a policy that encouraged the unlimited growth of exports, a policy that was very popular because it paid off and enabled the authorities to put off a number of delicate decisions, such as those concerning factory locations or business concentrations. The earliest difficulties seem to have arisen over the legal and customs consequences of joining the WTO, because they involved sacrifices.[5]

But the current problem is different, because the center is asking the provinces to rein in the pace of growth, to change its nature partially, and to repair the social and environmental damage they have caused. The response to this problem was at first negative, since the central policy was generally not applied. It was therefore necessary to hold a Congress of the CCP in 2007, the seventeenth, to impart more strength to the new policy, and in December 2007 a working session of the Central Committee laid out the duties of some and the threats hanging over others. What will be the results of this mobilization? Will it be possible to overcome established habits and accommodations? How will the new policy harmonize with the old principle that if the Chinese state wants to survive it has to authorize regional adaptations and local variations?[6] At the present time, it is impossible to answer these questions.

An All-Powerful but Aging Party

The claim to unity and the cellular reality of the country are both largely thanks to the fact that the CCP does not see itself as anything other than pan-Chinese but that it does not have the means to completely apply that model. This is one of the negative effects of its power, and it is not the only one, because everything indicates that the party has largely become an obstacle to the reforms it has claimed to embark upon.

The first reason for this is that the reaction to any possible economic difficulties and the development of social policies ought to be justified by the public welfare and not by an ideological goal, even that of a "harmonious society." The role of the state therefore should be reevaluated, which would call for a strengthening of the civil service. Change is in process in this area. Substantial pay increases have been granted to civil servants. The recruitment of state officials is increasingly done through high-level examinations, which could—theoretically—limit party intervention in appointments. These examinations are held after public notice for offices that are sometimes temporary. Employment for university graduates is now so scarce that the number of candidates is considerable, and the professional qualifications of civil servants are constantly improving.

Another positive change is that, with the burden of technical demands constantly increasing, specialized administrations have been cooperating more closely with professionals. The professionals have growing influence over the administrations, because the latter increasingly resemble embryonic corporations. More or less masked forms of cooperation have taken shape to the benefit of both parties. The administration of justice, for example, cannot do without judges, and the judges influence it, for instance by limiting the application of the death penalty: the recent decision to submit all death sentences to review by the Supreme Court is generally seen as a victory for the judges. Prosecutors for their part have increasingly succeeded in securing support from their administrations against the excesses of the security services. The administration is no longer the terrorized silent body of the Maoist period.

Yet despite this increased strength and the highly publicized recruitment of several noncommunist ministers and deputy ministers—this is far from novel—the leading role of CCP committees remains a universal fact. They play the preeminent role in ministries, including the Ministry of Justice and the Foreign Ministry. The change is that they are hiring into leadership positions more and more strong personalities who have become known for their professional abilities and who sometimes take original initiatives: we would say in the West that a number of these political figures in fact have administrative or technocratic credentials.

In addition, the rising importance of a genuine civil service implies a minimum of virtue and impartiality. It is on this point that corruption and the ensuing scandals have had their most pernicious effects. They arouse suspicions that often go far beyond reality: for example, the police are presented as universally corrupt, although on several occasions I have been able to verify the honest and efficient conduct of some officers. There is no doubt that the fight against corruption has been more vigorous and in any event more publicized since Hu Jintao came to power. In some administrations at least, there are even officials who are building their careers on a reputation for integrity, as in ancient times: cases of this have even showed up in rural districts. But it is still hard to estimate their number. In a regime that is at once monopolistic and firmly controlled by a plutobureaucratic class and in which everything begins and ends with money, the construction of a competent and impartial civil service is to say the least a complex enterprise.

But although the CCP still controls all the levers of power, its initiatives and practices increasingly vary depending on the sector, the location, and the administrative level, even on such sensitive subjects as urban planning, the protection of monuments, or the treatment of migrants: in those cases a variety of attitudes, or even of previously unthinkable opinions, is often displayed. Even on the most delicate questions of foreign policy—Japan, North Korea, Iran—political decision-making bodies are riven by sometimes very sharp disagreements. At the most delicate moments, some serving diplomats do not hesitate to air them and to comment on the rivalry between the principal factions in the Foreign Ministry.

Less monolithic, the party only exceptionally deploys its repressive operations and often limits its role of ideological mobilization to a bureaucratic ritual. Its propaganda leaves people indifferent, makes them smile, or annoys them, like the directive sent out during the Beijing Sino-African Conference in the fall of 2006, which suggested that the honorable African guests were divided between sex maniacs and dishonest consumers and promised that the party, otherwise so often indifferent to the fate of the poor, would cover unpaid bills: in the *hutongs*, many "comrades" were torn between alarm and anger. Except in localities where it is controlled by mafias, the party is no longer feared. In my street in Beijing, naughty boys openly made fun of the old militants who patrolled with their red armbands.

Another major development, fortunately countered in some places by the appointment of university graduates to responsible positions, is the institutional aging of an apparatus whose procedures have not changed for nearly sixty years. This aging is one of the explanations for the spatial cellular structure mentioned earlier. It explains in part the slow reactions of the apparatus when new threats surface—for example, the appearance of the Falun Gong sect in April 1999 or the SARS epidemic in the spring of 2003. It is also a cause of the fact that, at every level, party committees multiply commissions or ad hoc "leading small groups" to speed up their activity, but by doing so they also complicate it.[7]

In fact the only thing that really counts for the party, aside from "stability," meaning its own power, is economic growth. Other more "modern" duties, such as social equity and environmental protection, are only gradually finding a place on the agenda. The party is in the end a kind of bureaucratic concentrate of the plutocratic social stratum to which it has given rise.

A Bureaucratic Elite, a Cumbersome Apparatus

The CCP's social composition has adapted to the evolution of its duties. It used to recruit many common people that it then trained in blind obedience. Now it recruits primarily social climbers and those who have already arrived. One becomes a member of the CCP at the same time one gains access to other ways of obtaining money and social rank, or when one has put them together. For example, the party selects its future members among the most brilliant students—20 percent of the students of the famous Qinghua University, for example—or among a company's most deserving engineers and technicians. Being recruited by the party generally no longer means an ideological, still less a moral, commitment.

But anything can happen. There are still old nostalgic militants, often former workers in state-owned factories, who spend time together more to exchange memories of the great days, consult internal party journals at neighborhood committee offices on Sundays, and make up the slender audience for memoirs published by wives and secretaries of the great men of the regime. One also encounters technical officials excited by their profession and motivated by naïve party patriotism. And young people in China as elsewhere still have inexhaustible reservoirs of idealism: for example, a university professor recently told me that many graduate students asked to join the party to fight against poverty in China and the underdeveloped world.

Generally speaking, despite its size—seventy-two million members—the Chinese Communist Party is a party of elites. Only 32.5 percent of its members are peasants and 11.5 percent workers, and 30 percent have been to a university.[8] It has many professional officials—perhaps half its members. But it also has a significant number of company heads: according to a 2003 survey, a equivalent percentage of students in Beijing—62 and 60 percent—wanted to work in the private sector and to join the party.[9]

Compared to the great days of Maoism, the rising educational level and increasing concern with the economy are unquestionably positive elements. Engineering education was preferred during the first two decades of economic growth. It seems that legal degrees are favored today, which fits with recent attention paid to social questions: most new entrants into the Politburo have law degrees, including Xi Jinping and Li Keqiang, between whom the succession to Hu Jintao will be settled.[10]

However, for them as for most other officials, their time in school is moving swiftly into the past. Even at university, future leaders practice for bureaucratic duties: doctoral students chosen for a great career spend more time on "organizational" tasks than on their dissertations. Subsequently, former students soon become perfect apparatchiks, through careers that will have them circulate, depending on their initial rank, within a district, a city, a province, or the entire country and will develop in them very general qualities as well as membership in the microfaction and the network within which they are operating. In the Politburo, these generalist bureaucrats greatly outnumber those who also had a career in government. In contrast, a large majority have both experience and knowledge of the economic realm—qualities they also use to manage their own affairs. The combination of the characteristics of the apparatchik and preoccupation with private and public money indicates the fundamental duality of the social class in power.

Better educated than in the past, this bureaucracy is nonetheless just as cumbersome: the party and the administration continue to pile up billions of notes and to clog e-mail servers, because the efforts of successive leadership teams to promote a streamlined regime have failed.[11] The number of civil servants and officials continues to grow, and in 2005 they reached a record proportion of one out of every twenty-six residents of the country. The proliferation of positions is a known cause of slowness in making and applying decisions, but there are others just as well known, which provide fodder for newspaper cartoonists: the authoritarianism of ruling officials, competition between administrative systems and territorial districts, the inflation of propaganda, the doctoring of statistics. An honest district director, furious at not receiving the subsidy an international organization had assigned to him, traveled to Beijing one day to ask the organization in the future to deliver the money directly to him, in cash.

Overall, the Chinese Communist Party seems to have paid for positive changes—less violence, more competence—with two characteristics largely the result of its aging and that would reduce its ability to react in the face of difficulties: the decline of its efficiency and the cumbersomeness of its apparatus. There is another serious defect: its upper layers increasingly operate like a predatory aristocracy.

A Dangerous Aristocracy

To understand the danger this aristocracy represents, you must recognize that it is of political origin—it took shape in the highest levels of the post-Maoist CCP—and joined with the heads of major companies. It operates along family lines. In many cases, wives, mistresses, or relatives negotiate and collect the sums demanded.[12]

Several sets of great families have thus established themselves at the top of the system, and thanks to the political position of their heads, they have privileged access to important posts and wealth. For example, Hu Jintao's son, Hu Haifeng, runs a company that in 2006, by mere chance, won a contract to supply all the security scanners in Chinese airports.[13] Children of Jiang Zemin, Li Peng, Wen Jiabao, and of the great Chen Yun himself, one of the big five of the Mao regime, run important companies.[14] It seems that in the provinces as well other privileged circles have been established that are more or less connected to the aristocracy at the top.

To profit from its position, each family follows its own strategy, in which foreign missions and professional assignments play important roles. They choose important countries, English-speaking if possible, as well as vital professional sectors—for example, finance, transportation, and energy—or firms that depend on state contracts. But options may vary. For example, the family of the head of a city in Zhejiang chose Europe, with a presence in France and Great Britain, whereas many other families have chosen the United States.

The impression is that the predatory activities of the aristocrats and their clients have increased over the years. This is confirmed by a study showing that during the 1990s corruption did not so much increase in quantity as it "intensified"; that is, the major cases of corruption were the ones that increased the most.[15]

As in other privileged circles, a major problem is how to perpetuate advantages. In the Chinese regime, the solution is simple: political succession, cases of which are numerous and spectacular. Since the early 1980s, children of major leaders—known as "sons of princes"—have played major roles in directing the Chinese economy. For example, Chen Yuan, the son of Chen Yun, has held eminent positions in the banking system: assistant director of the Bank of China and then director of the Development Bank.

For a time, a certain discretion had been observed in political matters—even though Li Peng, prime minister in the spring of 1989, was an adopted son of Zhou Enlai. That time is long gone, however, and for a decade more and more "sons of princes" have appeared at the highest levels of power. Many of them hold significant provincial positions, nineteen were elected to the Central Committee by the Seventeenth Congress, and there are seven among the ten new members of the Politburo—among them the son of the first husband of Mao's wife Jiang Qing. At the highest level, although Zeng Qinghong, the son of an old companion of Mao, was forced to retire, the best-placed successor to Hu Jintao, Xi Jinping, is the son of Xi Zhongxun, a leader once purged by Mao Zedong who later played a considerable role in Deng Xiaoping's policy of opening. Some families are particularly powerful, like that of Deng Xiaoping: a daughter has recently been elected to the Central Committee. And the family of Zhao Ziyang, the successor to Hu Yaobang eliminated in 1989, who died in 2005, was able to negotiate the conditions of his funeral. To be persuaded of the power of the clan of Deng Xiaoping's heirs, one needs merely to glimpse the vast area it occupies along the superb Lake Houhai in Beijing.

To be sure, not all the members of this aristocracy deserve the feelings of fury they arouse in Chinese public opinion. I have met some of them, and they are charming and cultivated, and I have had the opportunity to witness the brilliance of Bo Xilai, the son of Bo Yibo, who, after a remarkable career, has recently become leader of the large city of Chongqing. Since they are already affluent, these "sons of princes" are probably not as greedy and more cultivated than the members of provincial aristocracies, who are currently in the process of establishing their fortunes. In addition, they apparently have not formed their own faction, because some of them are among the "Shanghai" faction, and others are among the associates of Hu Jintao. But the existence of an aristocracy of this kind seriously complicates the process of decision making and guarantees against excessively radical reforms.

Most important, the loyalty of its wealthiest members to their party and their country has been subject to doubt. Indeed, many of them—including, it is said, Li Keqiang's brother—have transferred their wealth abroad and later fled the country. It is estimated that tens of billions of dollars leave China illegally every year. According to a source in Hong Kong, 8,371 members and officials in the CCP and, according to a Japanese source, four thousand corrupt civil servants have left

China in recent years, taking with them $50 billion: first they have their wives and children leave, then they transfer their money, and finally they secure several foreign passports to choose from at the last moment.[16] The conduct of the aristocrats during the Asian financial crisis of 1997–1998 was not exempt from criticism and, during the SARS crisis of 2003, there was more alarm in those circles than in the rest of the population. In case of an economic crisis, it is probable that there will be further departures and massive capital flight—both facilitated by the fact that many sons of political leaders are business partners of multinational companies based in the United States.[17]

Is There a Pilot on the Plane?

The influence of the aristocracy is especially troubling, because it weighs directly on the head of the regime. It is said that its most important members, as well as those who knew him early in his career, do not hesitate to telephone him directly. They have contacts in Zhongnanhai, where the principal leaders and some widows of their great predecessors live: during the SARS epidemic, Hu Jintao's reaction was supposedly hastened by the fact that Chen Yun's widow's housecleaner was affected by the disease. In another example, Hu Deping, the son of the former General Secretary of the CCP Hu Yaobang, is a regular visitor to Hu Jintao, whom he knew well in the 1980s.

Hu Jintao will have to make difficult decisions, and he will have to display courage. But that virtue is the most dangerous and rarest in the history of the CCP. Hu's qualities are not in question. He has shown a good deal of lucidity and has been able to choose qualified experts to construct a program that is probably the best possible in the present "Chinese moment." His skill at maneuvering is also unquestionable: after being able to please all Deng Xiaoping's colleagues, he succeeded in imposing himself as the successor to Jiang Zemin in 1992, and after being able to last under Jiang he won the position, by a narrow margin, in 2002–2004.[18] During this period he reduced the influence of the "Shanghai" faction by obtaining the cooperation of Zeng Qinghong, a former loyal supporter of Jiang who controlled the administration of the Central Committee, but he then abruptly went on the offensive in the course of the Seventeenth Congress to get rid of Zeng.

What is in question is Hu Jintao's ability to make himself obeyed by his colleagues and the party apparatus. In fact, at the Seventeenth Congress he won only a narrow victory over the "Shanghai" faction and had to compensate for a victory in economic policy with a compromise on the identity of his successor. If the current hierarchical order is maintained, this will not be his candidate, Li Keqiang, but precisely the current boss of Shanghai, Xi Jinping, which casts doubt on the future application of Hu's policy.

That means that Hu Jintao still has to compromise with one of the most powerful factions that has ever appeared in the history of the People's Republic of China, that of Jiang Zemin. Based in Shanghai, it has been identified with the policy of giving priority to exports, which is now being challenged, because this policy places involvement in the world market above everything else and thereby protects the interests of "blue" China, that is, the lower Yangtze and the Chinese coast. In that, it more or less joins hands with another factionalism, which defends regional and provincial interests. This factionalism has not stopped operating in major and minor ways. On several occasions, for example, the northeastern provinces or those around Guangdong have joined together to secure advantages. On other occasions, more complex alliances have been manipulated in favor of or against a particular province: it appears, for example, that after the death of its most famous protector, Deng Xiaoping, several interest groups formed a league against the powerful province of Sichuan, which was considerably weakened by the loss of the city of Chongqing, which became a municipality directly administered by the central government and received significant resources. The regime's corridors bristle with hypotheses about analogous operations that are said to be aimed at other provinces or cities considered too powerful or too restive. As one might imagine, Shanghai is in the crosshairs.

It is still an open question whether Hu Jintao and his supporters will want and be able to defeat these two types of factionalism. All of them were originally connected to the Shanghai clan, with which they had made numerous compromises, and over the course of their careers they have formed other allegiances, particularly provincial ones. As soon as he was appointed by the Sixteenth Congress, Hu began to set up his own faction, luring several former Jiang supporters and fostering the rise of his men in provincial governments, military commands, and then in central bodies, which enabled him to break with some supporters and weaken others. At the present time, his faction consists primarily of his former colleagues in the northwestern provinces and in the Communist Youth League, graduates of Qinghua University, and alumni of the Central Party School, all places to which his career led him—but it is still relatively weak in military circles and in the richest economic regions.[19]

He also suffers from two serious weaknesses. For one thing, he is checked by the tendency of an aging party to allow a myriad of established positions to survive. The "internal democracy" to which Hu Jintao had to acquiesce at the Seventeenth Congress is in fact the slogan of the kingmakers—they are perhaps fifty in number—who intend to maintain control over supreme power.[20] Hu was forced to grant them substantial concessions, notably by conferring on the Politburo and its Standing Committee a role as executor of the decisions of the Central Committee. The future will tell whether this indicates an evolution toward a "consultative authoritarianism" and an "institutionalization without democracy" or, on the contrary, one of the episodes, frequent in communist history, in which a leader is reined in by his peers.

For another, Hu Jintao can only use weapons at his disposal with caution: the anticorruption police (because his own camp is not free of reproach), the press and public opinion (because he is not very democratic), the influence of "modern" professional bodies (because they would have to be rewarded in one way or another), and international opinion (because he also plays the nationalist card).

In the end, his only weapon—but it is a powerful one—is that there is no real alternative to the policy he proposes, at least at the present time, and no other figure has his status, particularly because he was anointed by Deng Xiaoping himself. This gave him his relative success at the last congress and will help to reinforce decisions made and to threaten offenders. But for the concrete management of affairs, it is to be feared that this weapon will turn out to be insufficient in an apparatus that is largely the prisoner of its own "society," that is, the plutobureaucratic class that has come out of the apparatus—and of the good will of its lower levels, particularly in emergency situations that would alarm established interests.

The Military Unknown

It is the relative modesty of the highest political authority that makes the question of the military troubling, particularly because of the dearth of information.

The proportion of the national income devoted to military expenditure has been rising for the last ten years after having substantially declined: the Chinese military budget, only a portion of which is public, is believed to be the second largest in the world, though it is still far below that of the United States.[21] The army's participation in power is still very favored: in 2007 the military made up only 2.2 percent of the membership of the CCP but 18 percent of the members of the Central Committee. But its role has diminished, and not only compared to the high point of the Maoist period. Indeed, since 2002, the army has had no representative on the nine-member Politburo Standing Committee, and in 2007 it lost its representative on the Secretariat of the CCP, whereas the general secretary of the party remains chairman of the powerful Central Military Commission of the Central Committee, which controls the army.[22]

At the same time, the army, still known as the Red Army, has been subjected to a twofold process of professionalization and technical modernization. Progress has been particularly noteworthy in the air force and the navy, and of course with respect to the most modern weapons: tactical and strategic weapons, war in space, electronic warfare. The Chinese army now has a second-strike capability from strategic submarines.[23] Generally speaking, it is moving away from its political, Soviet, and land-based traditions and coming ever closer to being a modern army.

Except that it has been on a war footing against Taiwan for sixty years. Its leaders use that as an argument for frequent budgetary increases. In addition, their responsibility for the Taiwan issue has sometimes led them to make very peremptory judgments about the way the civilian leadership was dealing with the question and to propose brutal solutions. For example, a superior officer threatened the United States with a nuclear strike if it were to interfere in the conflict. He was not publicly punished, which helps to maintain the mystery.[24]

A second particularity is that since the massacre of June 4, 1989, over which it had been given authority, the Chinese army has experienced increasingly open political discomfort. Its growing professionalization has led it to accept its subordination to the party rather than the state with greater reluctance. Moreover, it is annoyed at seeing its numbers decrease (a reduction by half in thirty years), the material difficulties of its members in a country where money is now the measure of all things, and the repeated need for difficult budget negotiations.

But Hu Jintao is in a weaker position than his predecessors in dealing with the army. Deng Xiaoping had the rank of marshal because of his service record. Jiang Zemin flattered the military and sometimes left the stage to them—for example, during the 1995–1996 military exercises against Taiwan. Hu Jintao is a pure civilian and does not always make the same effort. After the death of seventy men in a submarine accident in May 2003, he abruptly dismissed the commander of the navy and several other superior officers. At other moments, in contrast, he feels compelled to accede to the demands of the army. For example, the military budget was officially increased by 17.8 percent at the beginning of 2007, which made possible a rise of 150 percent in bonuses for officers. For its part, the army has apparently remained restive. In the months preceding the Seventeenth Congress, voices were raised in its ranks to demand that it be placed under the authority of the state.[25] Most important, it seems that on three occasions some of its leaders evidenced remarkable lack of discipline: first in October 2006, when a Chinese submarine came dangerously close to an American aircraft carrier; second in January 2007, with a sensational test firing on a Chinese satellite, when it "forgot" to have a very general authorization confirmed and to inform the civilian authorities on time;[26] and finally by providing technical facilities to some computer pirates, who attacked nerve centers of Western governments in June and July 2007.

Everything indicates that these initiatives provoked the anger of Hu Jintao. This was later confirmed by the change of twenty-five of the forty-two military members of the Central Committee decided by the Seventeenth Congress, as well as by the changes in the Central Military Commission of the Central Committee, notably the replacement of its vice chairman. These changes came on top of the transfers of five of the seven heads of the major military regions and the appointment of a new chief of staff.[27]

But everything is far from having been settled between civilian and military authorities. According to various sources, another Chinese submarine came very close to the American aircraft carrier *Kitty Hawk* in the Taiwan Straits in November 2007. During the same month, the great disorder triggered in the sky over southern China by military exercises conducted by the Chinese air force certainly did not suit the civilian authorities, less than one year away from the Olympic Games.[28] Let me be clear: the army is starting to be a problem in a regime whose civilian leadership has to some degree been weakened.

Chapter 7

One People?

BEING POORLY LED, THE CHINESE PEOPLE HAS BECOME HARD to govern. Since the waves of Maoist mobilization have stopped blending it together, it is no longer a single entity. Rather, it is the "heap of sand" that Sun Yat-sen deplored at the beginning of the twentieth century: it is following the same set of inclinations, of course—these days, profit and increased income—but is unable to cohere.

This is a fundamental point understood by people who have spent time in China: the Chinese people, reputed for its collective discipline, even for its nationalism, is not only diverse but is full of contrasts, contradictory, restive, and especially hesitant and unsure of itself. From a distance, the Chinese seem to resemble one another, to work together, and to be moving forward, whereas in reality they emphasize what differentiates them, they annoy one another, and they all dream of their own private schemes or of leaving the country. China is a large bed with a billion dreams.

A Detour Through Overseas China

Strangely, a helpful way of understanding the Chinese model's insufficient inclusiveness is to turn to what from a distance seems to be one of the jewels in the Chinese crown, the country's diaspora. The phenomenon is ancient—it apparently began early in the second millennium—and contrary to what we imagine, it says a good deal about the difficulty Chinese society has experienced in being what it believes itself to be.

Because emigration was usually caused by poverty, one imagines that once their fortune was made many émigrés returned to the mother country; this was true for only small numbers, especially because the empire theoretically closed its borders to returnees. No doubt the émigrés maintained an emotional tie to their native country, given concrete form in language and customs and sometimes a financial link—in the past to send assistance and now to invest, trade, and build a handsome family tomb in the home village. But, apart from a few visits, that's all.

With such different trajectories, the history of Chinese emigration is a history of frightful hardships and often persecutions but overall of remarkable adaptation to the receiving countries. We are surprised at the preservation of folklore in overseas Chinese communities. But their local integration is what really ought to impress us, along with the magnitude of their economic successes—not everywhere and not for all émigrés, of course. Those successes preceded that of the continent without spreading there: after 1978, overseas Chinese invested in the home country but did not return in force. At present, they are constantly adapting better to the receiving countries, using local law or custom to acquire the nationality of their country of residence, even in Japan. In the United States or Italy, they stand up for their commercial interests, if necessary with veritable riots. In Paris, the Chinese émigré community is considered to be one of the best organized.[1]

This does not mean that Chinese origin is a matter of indifference. Cultural and linguistic inheritances fade slowly, and effective mutual assistance groups are established, with models generally derived from the Chinese cultural repertory, that facilitate in many ways involvement in the economy of the receiving country. But these mutual-assistance groups are often based on local or dialect connections as much as on national origin. For example, in Southeast Asia and elsewhere one can find many "overseas Chinese" who are in fact primarily Hakka, Minnan, or Wenzhou (respectively from Guangdong, southern Fujian, and eastern China), most of whom do not speak standard Chinese. In other words, the reference to "China" is rather vague and generally more cultural than national: they are a diaspora that in the event of a military conflict involving their country of origin would likely feel less concerned than the Australians and Canadians did over the fate of England during the two world wars.

This detour through overseas China sheds light not only on relations between Chinese at home and abroad but on those connecting the metropolitan Chinese to one another: the bond among members of Chinese— or "pan-Chinese"—society is much more tenuous and fragile than is often acknowledged. "The Chinese" are an assemblage of many particles before being members of a single social body and citizens of a single national community. Although they claim to be members of that community and sometimes stridently maintain their "Chineseness," they all suffer from a form of separation or even exile in the face of the China that encompasses them.

An Unequal People

Inequality of conditions has always been a major form of that exile. The least that can be said is that the notion of equality has seldom been put forward in a Chinese society that classified its members in a hierarchical order and saw differences in condition as inevitable. In a way, communism conformed to this mania for classification by basing everyone's place in society on "class origins" and the distinction between urban and rural worlds. The criterion for inequality has partially changed, because class origin is little taken into account, but the difference between urban and rural citizens has merely been chipped away at, and money plays the primary role—which makes inequality less inevitable and less lasting, although just as visible. China is one of the most unequal countries in the world. Even more, it is a country in which until recently a vast majority of the population believed that inequality between individuals was not only inevitable but positive.

This is hardly surprising. The egalitarianism advocated by the Maoist regime had failed, and the primacy of private interests turned out to be more effective for economic development. This explains the enthusiasm with which many Chinese plunged into the search for individual profit. China is still a country in which you can meet at any time someone who will propose to you to establish a company; it is a country in which, until January 2008, it did not occur to an entrepreneur to offer his employees a labor contract or to many of his employees to ask for one. But it is also a country in which every new legal provision gives rise to the establishment of a swarm of law offices specialized in the art of evading it. Every product marketed legally has counterfeit equivalents, millions of infants are victims of illnesses caused by the bad quality of the milk, and at the gateway to all of the major cities all the certificates you might need to survive in the city are for sale. It hardly matters that this means you are wronging someone else, or everybody else. Every man for himself—and at best for his family and his village, too. You are told bluntly that this is the price to be paid to emancipate every individual and thereby the country. And people mock those European countries whose economic growth is sagging under the burden of social spending, that is, the impossible dream of equalizing conditions.

Yet, with time, a shift is becoming perceptible. The advantages of the richest have become too visible and have triggered jealousy. In addition, the generation that has swum so vigorously "in the ocean" of business has aged; it is preparing to retire and its members have started consulting doctors, meaning that they require increasing social protection. For all? Yes, for all people in cities, but the question of whether peasants deserve civilization has not yet been settled. The central authorities have perceived this aspiration, and they also want to establish a consumer market. They are therefore preparing to distribute guarantees and social assistance to city dwellers. For that reason, inegalitarianism has become a little more discreet.

But it survives in another way, which is geographical, because in such a huge country, individual connections are not only social but local. By dint of considering an impossible space unchangeable, the Chinese have set at the center of that space difference and indifference. The inegalitarianism of contemporary China is much more the effect of indifference to those who are unseen and unknown than to the fate of impoverished neighbors, who are beginning to become of concern. The greatest inequalities are geographical. Coastal regions have the highest living standards and receive 85 percent of foreign investment. The poorest regions are those of the interior, particularly in the mountains and on the edges of deserts, far from view.

In this regard, the mediocre results of the policy of developing the west launched with great fanfare by Jiang Zemin in 2001 are significant. The few industrial parks and development zones—occupied notably by foreign companies that wanted to get into the good graces of the Chinese authorities—have had much less success than had been hoped.[2] This has nothing to do with other operations in which the regime has invested more money because they satisfy its desire for prestige and profitability, such as the great Three Gorges Dam on the upper Yangtze, the new port of Tianjin, or the Olympic venues in Beijing.

An Inadequate State

The failure of the spatial equalization of conditions is partially explained by the state's inadequacies. In theory, a strong state possesses four characteristics: an ideology of the public welfare, complete control over its territory, an independent bureaucracy, and a direct relationship with its citizens. The empire, the nationalist regime, and the communist regime were unwilling or unable to meet these four goals simultaneously. As a result, the political authority was alternately too strong and not strong enough, and China oscillated between hypercentralization and disorder, between unity and division—in recent decades, constitutional and legislative variations have been constant. In addition, the intermediate space between the central government and local authorities has contained frequent variations of administrative levels and territorial districts. Overall, China has long been more an aggregation of localities than a society, more a society than a country, more a country than a state.

Is this formulation still relevant at a time when public policy has come to the fore? Not completely. One of the most important characteristics of the contemporary "Chinese moment" is the almost vegetable growth, from everywhere and nowhere, of something resembling the outline of a state. Think about it: the ideas of common growth, sharing the wealth, and environmental protection have given substance to the concrete claim of defending the public welfare; the territory is under better control than it has ever been, particularly thanks to the new means of communication; the administration shows some tendency toward strengthening; and finally, as I have pointed out, taking into account individual producers and consumers as participants in an economic pact with the authorities prefigures—faintly, to be sure—citizenship. This development discredits the frequent claims that the Chinese political sphere is forced into immobility by a power structure hanging onto its advantages. It is in fact evolving in a way that, without alarming the "owners" of the regime, might end up—it will take time, because the party is firmly in place—giving birth to a stronger and more impartial state.

Yet would this sort of evolution be sufficient were serious difficulties to arise? That is far from certain. The ideology of the public welfare is still polluted by the smoke of the great totalitarian blaze, and it is further compromised by the cronyism of those who extinguished it. Control over the territory is more a reality at the borders than in the interior, where, as I have noted, space is ever more cellular. However strengthened the state bureaucracy may be, it is still dominated by the party at every level. Even more important, the party is the spinal column of a society of privileges with an aristocratic society at the top, which bars the state from any universality and the "citizens" from any equality. Finally, if what permits the evolution is the fact that it is unspoken, this also acts as a brake on that evolution. It changes the relation of individuals to the authorities, but it does so implicitly and therefore does not provide the language for a new kind of relationship between individuals.

This is what is still weakening the Chinese state: it is practically without citizens. Citizenship requires at a minimum equality between citizens, the exercise of certain rights associated with nationality, and free participation in civic activities. Putting it mildly, civic equality is incomplete in China. The population is divided into two worlds, the city and the country; the former permits but the latter does not, or does very little, access to housing and the most modern professions, to money, and to travel. Only inhabitants of the first world can be citizens, but the twofold caste of party members and the wealthy have many ways of avoiding the duties associated with citizenship. There are thus both subcitizens and hypercitizens. That is especially true because peasants have no way of compensating electorally by their numbers for their inferiority to city dwellers. Hence the paradox of a state that is progressing, broadening its tasks, and trying its best to fulfill them, but a state that lacks partners and intermediaries in a social body torn apart by differences and inequalities. How can it secure obedience? In other latitudes, there remains the appeal to nationalism. In China, despite appearances, that is an illusion.

Vanishing Nationalism

Yet nationalism constantly makes its voice heard and sometimes becomes strident. Since the mid-1980s, agitation has been rampant among students and inside the party, forcing the leadership sporadically to take tough diplomatic stances.[3]

The country's foreign partners are particularly sensitive to these sudden shifts, because they understand Chinese communism as the product of a nationalist and anti-imperialist tidal wave. It is hardly an exaggeration to say that the most dedicated proponents of Chinese nationalism live outside the country. Regardless of the correctives and recent revelations by historians about the other reasons for success, the troubling (to say the least) conduct of Mao, and the nationalism of his rivals during the anti-Japanese war, the conventional wisdom is that now that its communist ideology has weakened, the regime retains a legitimacy based on nationalism. Had Mao not broken with the Soviet masters? Has Chinese foreign policy since then not always pursued the national interest? Is China not increasingly playing the role of a great power on the world stage?

This consensus is too simple a view. It would be easy to show that after 1949 nationalism played a variable and not always essential role in Mao Zedong's policies. Thereafter, Deng Xiaoping intelligently looked to the West for the technical and political means for development, and, aside from the mistake, more imperialist than nationalist in any case, of the failed offensive against Vietnam in February and March 1979, he was able both to drive and control carefully the rise of China in the world arena. No doubt, nationalist disturbances were manifest beginning in the mid-1980s, particularly in the universities. But they have remained limited. As a whole, this period has been the most effectively and least dangerously nationalistic one in recent Chinese history.

But things got complicated in 1989. After the June 4 massacre, the central government found it useful, to strengthen its failing legitimacy, to launch a "campaign for education in patriotism." It thereby encouraged the development of a populist nationalism that later surfaced on several occasions, in part because it was fed by the fears aroused by the deepening of China's opening to the world.[4] Thus was organized a spectacular show that was in part virtual, involving the confrontation between two contradictory and interdependent tendencies, one favoring and the other opposed to the opening.

For one thing, the way the opening is used by the elite in power fosters legitimate suspicions in the population. Isn't this just a policy that favors the rich, even when it claims the opposite? Who can believe that those working with foreigners don't take advantage of that to use their privileges to advance their own business affairs? Can anyone believe that big business battles concern the future of the country? The boss of the Wahaha firm, Zong Qinghou, is fighting Danone's "imperialism" in China, but a large part of his fortune is invested in the United States, and he is not the only one in that kind of situation.[5] The suspicion easily spreads to the government's diplomatic activity. In the end, doesn't protecting the business of Chinese capitalists consist of collaborating with the great powers, primarily the United States, and even with the sworn enemy Japan, to the detriment of the interests of the Chinese nation and, in particular, of the sacred duty to recover Taiwan?

To maintain appearances, the government authorizes outbursts of nationalist fervor, for example against the United States in May 1999, after the bombing of the Chinese embassy in Belgrade, and against Japan in April 2005. Then it swiftly returns to the original line: first because the leaders are privileged people who are anxious to maintain their access to Western conveniences or who are mandarins suspicious of popular irrationality, but also because they are aware that Chinese nationalism is askew. They recognize its central contradiction: it is a nationalism of people prepared to flee the country.

Many "returnees from the United States" claim to be violently anti-American, but the very ones—students, for example, and a large majority of urbanites—who react the most strongly against the excesses of the opening are viscerally tempted by the West. They dream of emigrating to the United States, save money to travel to Europe, and passionately looked forward to the Olympic Games. They would emigrate en masse if they had the opportunity.

One of my greatest surprises was to realize that there are huge numbers of Chinese who want to go abroad because they have no confidence in the future of their country and idealize the West. Consider: a Chinese Web portal asked browsers whether in some other life they would like to be Chinese. Sixty-four percent answered in the negative. Other surveys of students or schoolchildren produced analogous results.[6] For a year, I questioned all the taxi drivers in Beijing when the trip was long enough. I asked them if they would go to the United States if they (but not their family) were given a visa and a work contract: only one said no.

So there are two symmetrical sets of hesitations with regard to foreign countries: among the top leadership, between state politics and class politics, and in the urban population, between passionate adherence to the society of the masters of the world and the refusal to submit to it. These hesitations arouse reciprocal suspicions: in the population, the suspicion of betrayal by the leaders, and in the upper spheres suspicion of the irresponsibility of the masses. These suspicions are indeed quite plausible: it is impossible to avoid thinking that serious political and economic difficulties would severely test the national loyalty of the elite and the tranquility of the population; flag-waving demonstrations by the people and tough diplomatic stances by the elite badly conceal the ambivalences and hesitations of both. The least that can be said is that Chinese nationalism remains to be constructed and that at the present time it is hardly able to palliate the fragilities of the Chinese "national" community.

Chapter 8

Will China Finally Discover the World?

THE FIRST AND PROBABLY THE MOST IMPORTANT IDEOLOGICAL revision that took place inside the Chinese Communist Party had to do with China's relationship to the outside world. Consider: from the beginning of the Sino-American dialogue in 1971–1972, the leaders in Beijing were one after the other convinced that differences in political regimes did not always bring about hostility, that international trade can be a way of reducing divergences between countries, that participation in the process of globalization does not necessarily condemn China to marginalization, and that approval of Asian regionalization does not necessarily contradict the emergence of Chinese power.

In addition, having stopped being dangerous, the external world has become a constant frame of reference for all Chinese urbanites. They compare everything about their country to its foreign equivalents. They are fully aware of the vast backwardness of their living conditions. The public is passionately interested in the flash and gossip of the West and its stars: in November 2007, the Chinese media were less interested in Nicolas Sarkozy's diplomatic mission to China than in his divorce, and particularly in the unbelievable departure of Cecilia—is it legitimate for a wife to leave a president? The general public is also aware of all the small and large weaknesses of our systems: how could a former president of the republic be threatened with legal proceedings? More and more people can no longer imagine restricting their lives to Chinese horizons alone. On the contrary, they want to travel abroad and, why not, if the opportunity arises, settle there. One effect of the relative weakness of nationalism in the country is that the Chinese population is internationalizing itself with the same ease it once showed in bearing up under its isolation.

This extraordinary change is the logical consequence of the commercial and financial extension of China into the world. This is a remarkable result, one acclaimed by the press. Yet the party has remained surprisingly quiet on the subject. When it cannot avoid it, it presents economic successes as attributable to the intrinsic qualities of a regime or even of a people and a culture. The subject is basically a touchy one, because in reality these successes are largely thanks to the exploitation of an underpaid work force and wholesale collaboration with Western capitalism. In addition, privileges, trafficking, and shady deals are legion. The result is that the dogma no longer contains any analysis of the Chinese economic triumph and its consequences. It applauds the progress of relations with the rest of the world but does not define its meaning.

A Distorted View of the World

Because they have not analyzed their successes, the Chinese authorities have been unable to detect in time the mistakes in their approach to the external world, mistakes that are not lacking. Advise anyone who wants to be persuaded that nothing has changed in China to go to Beijing to ask about the country's foreign relations. They will meet intelligent professionals who, with grave intensity or jovial assurance, will utter the most conventional platitudes or even tell lies. This is enough to make you get on the first plane out. There is nothing surprising about this: in this area, unlike others such as the economy or sociology, research is tightly controlled by the major civilian and military organs of foreign policy, which means one has to know the language to detect the nuances of what is being said, and the press is either slavish and not very interesting or (like the well-known magazine *Time of the Planet*) simply nationalistic.

Yet even ill-intentioned visitors come back happy, because their interlocutors generally express an optimistic or even cheerful view of the world. They have tried to doubt, of course, the scripted speeches that they were given, but they had to concede that they were usually delivered sincerely. A happy surprise, because, after all, China would have good reason to complain about many of its foreign partners, who once participated in its dismemberment and then fought after 1949 against the new People's Republic. But what is impressive is the absence of rancor against all of them except Japan. It is even hard to remember that not so long ago China and the United States were at war over Korea and then confronted each other indirectly in Indochina. The French ought to be surprised that mention is seldom made of the long period when their country claimed to be the protector of Christians, its ships anchored in Chinese ports to respond with cannonades to incidents provoked by muscular preaching of the Gospel. Forgetfulness or politeness (rather than forgiveness) explains why Westerners in China are greeted with friendliness and kindness. Both obviously come from the fact that the external world has become a resource for the country. The same reason explains why there is nonetheless a drawback: the presence of any Westerner must benefit China. When that line is crossed because of a disagreement, a mistake in etiquette, or (say) an automobile accident, kindness dissipates, and suspicion, sometimes xenophobia, soon shows its face.

On the other hand, the Chinese view of the world suffers from two spectacular biases. The first is a fanatical fondness for hierarchy, for classification. It is hardly an exaggeration to say that the Chinese view the world the way sports fans in the West comment on soccer championships. There are the first-division teams and the others. Among the best, those at the top of the ranking are those comprising the United States, from the western states to the eastern ones, followed by the teams of Australia, Canada, and northern Europe, with a special place for France, which is capable of the best and the worst, and finally the teams of Eastern Europe and the Russian world. Behind them, the teams of the developing world fill out the bottom rungs, ranked in order of increasing skin pigmentation and decreasing per capita income.

A second bias, derived from the first, is the Chinese overestimation of the Western world. The country considered the most Western of the West, the United States, is an object of attention simultaneously passionate and jealous. China admires everything about the United States, except its foreign policy, on which it focuses hatred mixed with healthy caution, which is itself the product of its admiration—the Chinese public has never understood why a small European country like France took the risk to seriously displease Washington in the Iraq affair. America is both an ideal and a privileged adversary, and one sometimes gets the impression that the goal is to devour it in order to replace it.

Except for powerful Germany, European teams arouse limited but sympathetic curiosity. They are conquered markets and guardians of cultures worthy of being compared to Chinese culture, cultures that, at moments, are capable of some romantic flashes and technological successes. But even so, the appointment of Dominique Strauss-Kahn to the head of the IMF provoked some stupefaction—a Frenchman appointed grand financier of the universe!

The great victims of this classification are the developing countries—contempt for the Muslim world is overwhelming: many Chinese still believe that only the CIA could have carried out the attack on the Twin Towers in September 2001. The poorest countries of the global South are considered clients—in the past political and now economic, if they have raw materials. It was not in a Chinese but in a Japanese university that I attended a conference on "Africa 2020," which explored the hypothesis of the appearance on that continent of one or more development centers: that hypothesis would seem zany in China. Even stranger in fact is the secondary status still assigned to major emerging countries such as Brazil and especially India, which, for keen observers, is China's real rival in "the match of the century."[1] The attention the Chinese media outlets give to India is both limited and distracted, despite recent progress, and research on contemporary India is decades behind the world standard.

The Chinese view neglects or underestimates both the latent possibilities of poor countries and the complexities of strong countries. For example, with rare and brilliant exceptions, the history of the United States is practically unknown, and there is often no knowledge of the foundations of the political tendencies that are admired or denounced in stereotypical ways. The negative view of the older European countries relies on prejudices and denies them the very capacity that China is in the process of developing: to become "young" while remaining proud of their antiquity. And the difficulties of definition in the European Union are attributed to an essential ebbing of force, with no attention paid to the numerous difficulties of the immediate economic circumstances. This attitude leads to blunders when, miraculously, a European negotiator or leader shows talent or firmness. Beijing's impatience with the sonorous and powerful speech of Angela Merkel on the ethics of bilateral relations between states is an excellent example.

The Dangers of Pragmatism

When you know little, you move forward and learn from experience: in China, as elsewhere, distorted or inadequate knowledge leads actors to pragmatism. In this instance, Chinese pragmatism effectively links political and commercial offensives. Official missions precede and then support commercial offensives. Hu Jintao has traveled around Africa several times, and Beijing even sent the Sudanese authorities a mission of the CCP led by Zeng Qinghong himself: one wonders what ideological problems may have been addressed.

In this area, Beijing's two principles, so to speak, are "nonintervention in the affairs of states"—meaning the acceptance of all kinds of partners—and "cooperation"—which means seeking maximum material advantage, if necessary by granting substantial loans to poor countries intended to finance trade or construct the infrastructure needed to carry it out. In matters of trade, Chinese merchants rely as much as they can on their comparative advantages—low export prices, massive purchases of imports—and do not hesitate to buy at a high price. Diplomats and merchants take into account international conventions or rules, or even notifications of noncompliance, only if they are absolutely forced to. For example, the European Commissioner for Consumer Protection declared in November 2007 that in one-third of cases notified by Europeans, exports of products not meeting standards had been stopped, but in almost six cases out of ten no measures had been taken.[2]

In the current state of world society, these simple practices have produced noted successes that have led to important contracts for the supply of raw materials. But ignorance of the terrain has also produced failures. Both were particularly obvious in the well-known African offensive: trade practically tripled between 2003 and 2006, providing 33 percent of the tropical wood, 24 percent of the oil, and 22 percent of the diamonds needed by the Chinese economy—yet these imports were balanced by exports, which is a fine performance.[3] But the obstacles encountered are obvious: inadequate infrastructure, attacks on Chinese personnel, boycott campaigns, growing suspicion in ruling circles. The choice of partners was heavily challenged by Western public opinion. Eventually, China will have to improve its adaptation to the local territory if it wants to avoid limiting its ambitions.

Other incidents that have arisen in trade relations with Western countries have demonstrated a dangerous combination of naïveté and cynicism. There is, for example, the rejection by American, European, and Japanese importers of Chinese exports, particularly children's toys and food products, for quality defects. How could Chinese exporters not foresee that, since they were not without foundation, press campaigns against Chinese products would end up having negative results? The Chinese economy is now in danger of acquiring a disastrous reputation.

In addition, aware of the naïveté and gaps in knowledge of its partners, China has profited excessively from control over its own territory to trick them in a thousand ways. The narrative of these deceptions amuses connoisseurs and gives value to certain accounts.[4] The Western companies concerned have kept a discreet silence about the Chinese commercial opera often performed at their expense. But researchers will one day evaluate the unprecedented magnitude of the counterfeiting that has run rampant in China since the late 1980s: during the summer of 2006, only 9 percent of European companies established in Beijing said they had experienced no problems protecting intellectual property.[5] But Chinese counterfeiters would have been wrong to worry as long as Western officials bought fake Rolexes in the morning and then in the evening demanded the end of counterfeiting, or as long as one could see the wife of a president in Beijing buying quantities of fake Vuitton bags.

One day, there will also be an assessment of the thousands of methods used to siphon funds, goods, and techniques from foreign companies whenever they lowered their guard. We have seen fleets of automobiles emptied out, agreements urgently renegotiated because the Chinese partner threatened simply to disappear, police departments demanding thousands of euros to appease the "anger of the Chinese people" at a "rape" that was nothing but an ordinary love affair. We can add the thousands of practices designed to plunder the technology of "foreign friends" and to divert in favor of Chinese firms the protective legislation Beijing had been obliged to adopt: it still happens that foreign firms have their procedures stolen and then are found guilty of counterfeiting Chinese products. Forty years ago, young Chinese were taught that capitalism was theft: not everyone forgot the lesson.

One cannot fail to connect these mistakes to other imprudent actions committed in the political realm. Some are minimal though meaningful, like the declaration of a Chinese ambassador who contemptuously dismissed the position taken on Tibet by some local personalities, one of whom later became minister of foreign affairs. Some means used, as old as the world, make one smile: it is said, for example, that some generals have not resisted the charms of Beijing's female spies. Others are more dangerous: the Chinese technology espionage networks operate with very uneven discretion. Geng Huichang, the new minister of state security—often described as the Chinese KGB—is an expert in economic intelligence. American intelligence officials have complained that Chinese espionage operations are reaching "cold war levels."[6]

Naïveté of the Merchant, Vanity of the Mandarin

Facilitated by ignorance and naïveté (often of Western partners), mistakes and reckless actions in fact have two different sources, and these correspond to the two faces of China's rise in the world: one is mercantile, the other mandarin.

The international spread of Chinese "capitalism" has been heavily influenced by experience in China itself, where companies seldom risk real competition and operate under the shelter of political protection.[7] To say the least, Chinese capitalism is not accustomed to patience, caution, and concessions. Internationally, it therefore acts according to a very simple principle, which consists of using its comparative advantages as long and as thoroughly as possible, often by employing Chinese labor on site. It pays no attention to local facts and psychologies: it keeps accumulating profits as long as it can—isn't profit the law of the capitalist world? It carries on business the way Monsieur Jourdain spoke in prose.

In contrast, the conduct of diplomats evokes that of mandarins plunged into a different world against their will. Inexperience and lack of knowledge make for an understandable explanation. But like, although even worse than, Western diplomats, the mandarins sent by Beijing seldom mix with the local population, with very few exceptions. Their relations are sparse and stereotyped. With a few brilliant exceptions, specialists of the French-speaking world know only a little more than the others; this is not of great importance, because they limit their activity to a small perimeter around the embassy. They are unconcerned if they fail to attend a reception. They are the bearers of an entirely symbolic grandeur that is not worth risking. To keep informed, they read newspapers, but they ignore journals of opinion and everything that keeps a culture vital: they are never seen in the Latin Quarter or the neighborhood of the Bastille. It doesn't matter: they represent China and, if necessary, will go at the drop of a hat to the Foreign Ministry to berate the minister himself. They are disciplined, and in that sense they are effective—but not very attentive.

These two categories of actors, who frequent each other abroad even less than their French counterparts, share a surprising characteristic: they implicitly assume that being Chinese requires no particular precautions in today's world. This is incredible. These people were absent from our world for decades, and they returned as though nothing had happened. Not that they behave badly: far from it, because they are cautious and usually polite, but with rare exceptions, they feel no particular need to pay attention and take care. They are at ease in our countries, but they are hardly interested in us.

What If the World Stopped Welcoming China?

Their attitude, then, is as different as possible from the timid and awkward politeness of Japanese diplomats or the readily critical intelligence of the Indians. It is based largely on the implicit conviction that no foreign country is really opposed to China. Perhaps this idea comes from the naïve idea that societies governed by capitalism are somehow rigorously ruled by power. It appears that some Chinese are already savoring the delights of victory. They used to approach money with suspicion; now it motivates their confidence, which is just as naïve but more dangerous.

In any event, this attitude is imprudent, and it may lead to a rude awakening, first because their partners' ignorance will in the end dissipate, and all the difficult issues will be open for discussion—foreign investment in China as well as trade relations. The West will probably even exaggerate the difficulties it has long ignored—similar to the treatment of the issue of human rights in China, about which sensitive souls now wax bombastic in proportion to their earlier indifference. Company officials are already complaining that China is "more and more expensive." That's true, but only relatively speaking; it is also true that only recently have people made some calculations. And China is going to become a competitor of the West in areas involving the most sophisticated technology—and not just any competitor, but one that knows how to invest and has the resources to transform its economic successes into political power. It will then stop receiving subsidies, and its work will get harder.

Of course, that does not mean a complete reversal of directions is going to occur and that China could again find itself surrounded by a coalition of enemies. Whatever happens, China will remain necessary for world economic growth and world peace. It simply means that the country will be confronted with the problems it has neglected.

One of these is represented by the increasingly vigorous reactions of American economic officials. China is, of course, not defenseless. When Americans ask the Chinese to revalue the yuan and to stop counterfeiting, the Chinese can point to American companies that use Chinese territory as a low-cost workshop and can threaten to invest a growing portion of its surplus not in American Treasury bills but more profitably in other economies. To make this threat credible, it has recently established a sovereign wealth fund, which has already begun to operate. But the growing weakness of the American market is going to induce it to make more concessions. In any event, it will have to pay more dearly for the huge surplus it earns from the U.S. market.

The reaction will probably come later on with the European market, where, over time, by pitting European administrations against one another, China has succeeded in securing a 37 percent increase in exports and a surplus of almost $170 million in 2007. It now exports more to the European market than the United States and imports from it less than Switzerland. But here, too, it would be wrong to imagine that the European Union will not in the end wake up, that it will not oversee more carefully the application of its tariff barriers and will not demand the removal of Chinese non-tariff barriers—which cost them €20 billion annually. Sino-European relations have already encountered some difficulties, and not only on trade issues. A new generation of leaders has appeared—Angela Merkel, Gordon Brown, Nicolas Sarkozy— who are to varying degrees less well disposed than their predecessors toward Beijing.[8] So, even in Europe, China will have to be prepared to encounter firmer reactions that will require on its part much defter conduct.

As is often the case, the fears aroused by the emerging power of China are embellished with moral motives. It is criticized not for enriching itself but for doing so selfishly and unjustly. Indeed, it achieved economic takeoff without worrying about the fate of other countries, particularly the industrial sectors that its exports destroyed. Beijing can certainly put forward historical arguments showing that the powers that emerged first were precisely those that took no precautions; every takeoff occurs to the detriment of existing positions, and often by less than moral means. But the most effective response will be to change both the appearances and the realities lying behind these criticisms.

Despite its size, with respect to globalization China has long behaved like a stowaway: it profited without paying the price. This situation began to change only with its entry into the WTO. Since then, Chinese trade legislation has come closer to that of the rest of the world, its criminal law has evolved, and its diplomacy has cooperated in peacekeeping operations. But its political regime maintains an authoritarianism that seems shameless in the eyes of any democrat, and it takes advantage of all possible means to postpone the application of global norms. From this perspective, an essential issue is that of the environment. To assess its efforts, Beijing argues that the West has also delayed a good deal, which is perfectly true. But in the present situation, China has every interest in persuading the rest of the world of its goodwill and in showing that it is prepared to pay its dues for the maintenance of world order.

The Chinese leaders are beginning to see the problem. They realize that they ought to make themselves understood and, if possible, loved. To do this, they have decided to open around the world by 2010 five hundred "Confucius Institutes" intended to teach the Chinese language to one hundred million people. In addition, the national public television network, CCTV, which also has a good English-language station and has recently established another in French and Spanish, plans to create new ones in Russian, Arabic, and Portuguese by 2010. This is excellent news, but it will be no substitute for substantial changes.[9]

A Good Neighbor?

One of those changes would be to persuade the world that China can decently be counted among the "good citizens" of the planet, a country that does not threaten its neighbors. After all, a characteristic shared by all prosperous countries today is that peace reigns on their borders. But this is not completely true for China.

No doubt there has been remarkable progress since the 1970s, when there were problems on every border. The Russian border has been pacified since the early 1980s and its limits established by bilateral agreements. Relations between Beijing and Moscow are now troubled only by trade disputes, Russian protests over cross-border trafficking, and the activities of Chinese mafias in the far eastern border provinces of Russia. Within the framework of the Shanghai Cooperation Organization, the two countries control Central Asia and block American influence as well as Islamist groups and Uighur irredentists.[10]

In addition, the continuing improvement in relations with India since the beginning of the millennium and the recent upsurge in trade between the two countries—$40 billion in 2007[11]—allow for the hope of a lessening of tension over border disputes and, more important, the dissipation of mutual distrust, but this will take time and patience. And although Burma seems more and more afflicted by the yoke of the generals and little inclined to follow Chinese advice, the Burmese border is practically controlled by Beijing. Over the years, despite serious and persisting divergences over the status of disputed islands in the South China Sea,[12] Sino-Vietnamese relations have become peaceful, to the benefit of Chinese trade, and the influence of the great neighbor has been exercised without hindrance in Laos and Cambodia.

This new climate on the borders has been confirmed by a strategic revolution: China has become engaged in a genuine regional politics. Until the early 2000s, Beijing restricted itself to a collection of bilateral policies. It remained aloof from Asian regionalism, which it saw as bolstering Japanese influence and thereby American hegemony. These fears were dissipated by Japanese timidity, the concentration of American policy on terrorism and the Middle East, and the new importance of Chinese commercial interests. Beijing's diplomacy therefore changed direction and decided to contribute to the regionalization of Asia. It is participating fully in the political dialogue that has developed in the framework of the Asian Forum and the "ASEAN plus three." It has increased its number of bilateral economic agreements and signed an ambitious pact with ASEAN that provides for the establishment of a free trade zone from which Chinese exports will derive major profits. Thanks to this shift, China is in the process of imposing itself, at least temporarily, as the heart of the New Asia.

Despite this truly historic progress, three serious problems remain on the borders of China. The first one, North Korea, has temporarily subsided, but not necessarily for long and not necessarily to the benefit of Beijing. Exasperated by Pyongyang's blackmail and lying and for once mobilized not just by their security interests but also by their sense of responsibility—as well as by American pressure—the Chinese authorities reacted vigorously to North Korea's October 2006 atomic test. The sound of boots was heard on the Chinese side of the border, and Kim Jong Il feared for the independence of his dictatorship. He therefore allowed the Americans to dismantle his nuclear research facilities and initiated a new dialogue with South Korea. The international problem of the North Korean atom is fading, then—no doubt temporarily— but not the hostility, as ancient as it is discreet, between Beijing and Pyongyang.[13]

More broadly, however dynamic cooperation with South Korea may be—an entire neighborhood is being built in Beijing for several thousand Koreans, where Chinese officials will be expected to speak Korean—Chinese policy on the issue of reunification remains enigmatic. China, it seems, has not completely given up an imperial policy of division of the peninsula, which also lies behind its suspicion of American and Japanese influence.

Much more serious for its reputation are the problems raised by what can be called China's Japanese and Taiwanese "neuroses." Both are legacies of history, and they are partially connected by the fact that Taiwan is the only territory in the Chinese world that retains a rather positive memory of the Japanese occupation (1895–1945), and Japan does maintain close and substantial relations with its former colony. But these two neuroses are very different.

Summarizing roughly, Japan is a neighboring state much smaller than China, and it owes much of its culture to China. However, it has made the mistake of succeeding in everything—except during World War II—whereas China has failed in everything, at least until recent decades. Japan's economic triumph long seemed unjust to many Chinese. In addition, Japanese aggression has left appalling memories that the considerable aid provided to Beijing since 1978 has not appeased, especially because Tokyo chose to remain under American protection. On the contrary, the successors of Mao Zedong and Deng Xiaoping, with less of an aura from the legends of war, thought it necessary to maintain the popular resentment against Japan at a time, moreover, when Tokyo was beginning to assume its new status as a major power and to grow impatient at Chinese rebuffs. The conflict surfaced starting in 2001 over the visit paid annually by Prime Minister Koizumi to the Yasukuni Jinja, the shrine for heroes who died in World War II, among whom are war criminals. This provided an outlet for popular nationalism in China and legitimated China's blocking of Japan's candidacy for permanent membership on the Security Council. It should be pointed out, however, that more moderate tendencies have never stopped operating in Chinese diplomatic and intellectual circles.[14]

Anti-Japanese demonstrations were finally authorized, if not organized, in April 2005, and they brought about several months of bilateral tension, under circumstances in which the two navies frequently crossed paths in contested waters. The episode revealed such popular hostility to the Chinese authorities and was so harmful to bilateral economic exchanges and to China's international reputation that the more moderate tendency gradually resumed control in Beijing, and in Japan, Koizumi was replaced by advocates of compromise. The authorities in Beijing put an end to the demonstrations and in 2007 gradually restored cordial relations with the Japanese government, although they did not specifically announce regret for the incredible excesses of language that their propaganda had authorized.

The Taiwan question is also a humiliating matter for Beijing. This island of twenty-three million inhabitants has unquestionably been part of the Chinese world since the eighteenth century, but it has had a specific fate. It underwent a long Japanese occupation, followed by a seizure of control by the nationalist troops of Chiang Kai-shek retreating from the continent in the late 1940s. This was in turn followed by economic development largely generated by proximity to Japan and then, starting in the late 1980s, by a process of democratization. Finally came a rise in demands for independence. For China, Taiwan's economic triumph represents a humiliation, because it provokes unpleasant comparisons. Its de facto independence is evidence of China's weakness as well as a threat to its security, because it is guaranteed by American protection. And its democratization is a sharp political contradiction as well as a seductive example for the population on the continent.

These two problems are extremely harmful for the Beijing authorities, not only for security reasons. As comprehensible and legitimate as some of China's historical arguments may appear in both cases, they have two major weaknesses. The first is that the People's Republic is a communist dictatorship, whereas Japan and Taiwan are peaceful democracies. That is enough to discredit Chinese fury against Tokyo's alleged "militarism" and Beijing's intent to bring under its wing a Taiwanese population that has often made its intentions known at the ballot box. The second is that the attitude of the Chinese authorities to their two neighbors has appeared to be unevenly rational. It is as though these two problems took on a partially neurotic aspect after Deng Xiaoping left power in the early 1990s. To say the least, Beijing's language contains or authorizes obvious excesses, unquestionable mistakes (such as the tripling of the real number of victims of the Nanjing massacre in December 1937), and insults that otherwise have become rare these days in international relations.

The Chinese government is probably less unanimous than it appears to be on these two questions. Many leaders are convinced that Japan is a necessary economic partner—even if its ambition to become a permanent member of the Security Council has to be countered. Some of them also seem convinced that the smartest solution to the Taiwan issue is to reduce the range of its actual independence and to tie it to the Chinese economy, which would make the use of force unnecessary. But the Chinese government considers it impossible to abandon its "right" to use offensive means, which would leave open the possibility of a military accident. In addition, it is not certain that it fully realizes the mistake represented by its encouragement of the wave of nationalistic populism. In short, in this area as in others, the unquestionable progress achieved has not abolished all anxiety.

Chapter 9

What Does China Want?

A Harmonious Society?

IT REMAINS TO DETERMINE WHAT PROGRAM FOR THE FUTURE the leaders are really proposing to the population. As of now, there are two clear and more or less consensual goals: raising living standards and increasing the country's power. After the end of the Maoist nightmare and in the ensuing era of prosperity, that alone was enough to make sense.

But a minority of the urban population has already attained what the government nicely calls a "society of small prosperity." It now has other concerns, ethical, metaphysical, touristic. This is the group that comprises the numerous readers of books rehabilitating Confucianism. If growth stalls, the advance of the rest of the population toward that "adequate comfort" will be slowed, and accessing power will seem harder to accomplish. Other goals will therefore have to be found.

The country's current leadership seems aware of the problem and appears to be trying out two solutions. One consists of liberating nationalistic passions. In Beijing's alleys, you can often hear that China not only has to succeed in organizing the Olympic Games but that it also has to win the largest number of medals, and that if the government really wants to please the people, it should invade Taiwan without delay. With the expectation of having to meet the first challenge—and unable to rise to the second—the government made a gesture by authorizing the anti-Japanese incidents of the spring of 2005, but those too had their drawbacks. This is why the center seems inclined to propose a second solution, the creation of a "harmonious society."

This concept does have two major advantages. The first is that by evoking Confucianism it provides a way out of leaden Marxist discourse. For that reason, Hu Jintao did not succeed in having it included in the party statutes at the Seventeenth Congress of the CCP. But this also allows it to be made into a goal for everyone, valid for both domestic and foreign policies. The second advantage is that while responding to demands of a moral order, it satisfies objective requirements that fit in with the logic of the country's development. After building new cities, China has to provide them with social and cultural services. After increasing income, it has to make the lives of producers secure and increasingly turn them into consumers.

This project is both coherent and reasonable. It meets real needs and can serve as the basis for a new and eventually more explicit contract between the regime and the population. In principle, it can speed up the construction of a more solid and universal state. This is why the slogan has been accepted. Many members of the party see it as being in salutary conformity with social goals that have been too long subordinated to productive goals. The population sees in it an at least indirect acknowledgment of the current regime's flaws and at best a promise for the future.

Yet in both categories the "harmonious society" is seldom mentioned without irony. Why? It is an indication of a surprising fact: many Chinese have little confidence in the capacity of their country to transform itself into a great modern nation. They do not like it when foreigners list the obstacles along their path, but they willingly bring them up themselves: the size of the population, the lack of discipline, the egotism of the rich, demographic evolution. Newly converted to the market economy, they are the first to be convinced that the available budget will never satisfy needs: how can you finance retirement pensions in a society that will soon have one worker for every four old people? But they have nonetheless not forgotten the articles of faith they used to recite by rote, and they draw a fatalistic conclusion from their experience: no growth without capitalism, but no justice with it.

Dialogue on Confidence in and Mistrust of the Communist Party

Generally, at this stage of the discussion a sledgehammer argument comes to the fore: how can we trust "them"? How can we trust the corrupt, the monopolists, that is, the party officials? I usually reply that the population was, all things considered, right to have confidence in Deng Xiaoping's development policies. But I am told that, at the time, officials wanted to develop the country to enrich themselves. I respond that since they were more intelligent about this than were the ruling classes in a number of developing countries, they probably understand that the satisfaction of the people's needs is a condition for keeping the CCP in power. I'm wasting my breath: for many of my interlocutors, the enrichment of party officials through corruption was the purpose, the alpha and omega of economic policy. Moreover, in their view, the possibility of political change is unlikely not only because of the regime's inherent power but especially because of the fragmentation of popular aspirations.

This dialogue is not imaginary. I have experienced it in whole or in part with many Chinese in all walks of life, including members of the party. In my view, it provides two major lessons. The first is that corruption, and more generally the moral decadence of the plutobureaucratic class, is probably more serious for the future than for the present. Indeed, it leads one to think that the only desirable course is the indefinite continuation of the hyperproductive present, which leaves some leftovers for the lambs after the wolves have fed themselves. For how is it possible to believe that the wolves would behave better if the provisions were less abundant?

In the present "Chinese moment," this sort of dialogue can be conducted in the open, because it implies that the government's goals are just but that the conditions for accomplishing them are lacking. But in discreet private conversations, more radical arguments are added on, calling the Chinese Communist Party into question: it has never been concerned with the life of the people but simply seized control. In the past, it enjoyed its power. Now, it enjoys the wealth that power provides. Speeches about the "harmonious society" are like the old ones about communism, mirages designed to facilitate the manipulation of minds and bodies. This language, as questionable as it might seem, is more widespread than it appears, even in the countryside, where change is least visible: after all, today like yesterday, peasants live under the iron rule of petty local chiefs. By refusing to change its name, mode of operation, and habits, the CCP provokes among the masses deep suspicion whenever it proclaims a change that would not primarily serve the party itself.

Thus the new goal that the Chinese leadership claims it is pursuing suffers from a great lack of credibility. This lack is probably not permanent by nature. The government would no doubt be more likely to persuade the people if it rapidly implemented multiple significant social projects throughout the territory, projects of the kind that already exists in large cities and rich areas: superb cultural facilities, experiments in social services, trial implementation of pension systems. But its cautious empiricism—which is perhaps also a reflection of the indifference of its constituents—is likely to reduce the strength of its convictions. The "harmonious society" is in danger of remaining a piece of propaganda or a nostalgic dream.

Conclusion

China's Great Challenge

IN 2006, WHEN I BEGAN TO THINK ABOUT WRITING THIS BOOK, foreign commentators did not believe in the possibility of a Chinese crisis, much less that one was imminent. Yet Chinese leaders were constantly sounding the alarm, in vain. By early 2008, however, the climate had changed, first of all because Chinese economic circumstances themselves had changed. In the face of the return of inflation and the decline in American imports, some hasty commentators even began to panic. Later, it was because the authorities' directives intended to reduce growth had begun to be applied. Had they cooled off the economy too much? In any event, for the first time in a long time, it had become fashionable to foresee a recession in China.

A recession is likely, but its seriousness is unpredictable, and in any event its consequences will be even more important, because it would signal the end of the period in which the legitimacy of the government and the confidence of the population depended on rapid growth. A great challenge would face the country: the challenge of inventing the future.

The Question of the Future

It may sound banal, but for this country the problem is not. Indeed, it was economic growth and its benefits that reconciled the great mass of the Chinese to a collective future. Previously, the brutality with which Mao Zedong constantly afflicted it had led the population to turn in on itself. In the face of the harshness of the present and the absurdity of the obligatory future, the only thing valued, along with present personal affections, was the memory of lost happiness. Never had ancient currencies, old photographs, and books from other times been so carefully preserved as when it was forbidden to do so, in the 1950s. Almost everything was destroyed in the end during the Cultural Revolution, but it did not disappear from thought. Quite the contrary, particularly in the countryside, one witnessed a dramatic revival of superstitions and old beliefs.

Everything changed in the early 1980s, when economic growth restored interest in the present. And then gradually the successes of the new economy restored the credibility of a better future for everyone— or almost everyone. Strengthened by the duration of the period of growth—soon it will be three decades—the Chinese became used to anticipating that tomorrow would be better than today. When major infrastructure projects and the construction of the Olympic stadiums began, the future took its place in the heart of the present, until the two became one.

As a result, the end of the perpetual "great leap" in income has every disadvantage. It compromises the idea of a present better than before, and, even more, it places in doubt the compensation of the present by the future: the decline of the present makes the future opaque. How can one project oneself into the future when it has stopped being in some sense palpable, visible?

Yet the event would have one advantage. The decline of the present makes the only possible and attractive future a different future: in this sense, it liberates the future. And even better, a future really different from the present could be found only in the rediscovery of the past. For that future to deserve a commitment of will, it would have to refer to a credible past, one no longer partial but complete, one no longer stereotyped but encompassing all human experience, in short a past freed from official lies and lazy popular thinking. The decline of the present could therefore engender or facilitate the rediscovery of history. China will be able to reinvent itself only if it begins by rediscovering itself, not only in the glorious operas of its official past, but in its excess and pettiness, its lies and mistakes. And in its modern tragedies, in particular those of the terrible twentieth century. It will be necessary to take the old photographs out of cupboards and allow the dead to speak. What did they die from? What did they die for?

Toward Modernity?

For the moment, unfortunately, the Chinese authorities are not prepared to open their archives and are thus limiting contemporary Chinese history to shapeless and faltering attempts.[1] Does this reflect obstinacy, caution, or developing pragmatism?

But they do seem to have worked out a fairly coherent definition of a different future, one that would enable them to stay in power. In the first place, and this is of some significance, they have understood that the range of choices open to them, once so exaggerated by Mao Zedong, has been further reduced by globalization. What this forces countries like China that want to play a prominent role to adopt is modernity, meaning they must reach the highest level in the world. This was already the path chosen by Deng Xiaoping when he promised "four modernizations": of industry, agriculture, science, and defense technology, all areas necessary for the survival and strengthening of the country. Once a first program was fulfilled, the goals were expanded. They have been broadened to include the social distribution of progress and environmental protection. This represents a formidable wager that would turn a dangerous phenomenon—reduction in the rate of growth—into a means of progress: the construction of a consumer society, technologically, culturally, and socially modern, built in a "scientific" way, which would become a "harmonious society" without going through democracy.[2]

With the Cultural Revolution, Mao Zedong claimed to be making out of contradictions, at the time relatively rare and weak, the source of revolutionary renewal. This time, the issue is to make a society harmonious that is anything but and to cause China to advance toward a sort of peaceful model, in which the informed activity of the party-state would abolish the contradictions that cause violence. On paper, this project thereby offers a response to the most dramatic problems of Chinese politics: the lack of popular trust, social inequality, the lack of confidence in a party-state, and hence its dramatic authority deficit.

Difficult "Harmony"

But Hu Jintao's project seems to suffer from a form of idealism exactly the inverse of that of Mao Zedong. By raising contradictions, Mao intensified and diffused them. Hu Jintao does not acknowledge them and hopes to make them impossible. But reality is stubborn. Contradictions will threaten the "harmony" so exalted by propaganda. Not only do they exist, but they will inevitably be accentuated or multiplied by inescapable factors. The first has to do with the resources available for policies that will be incredibly costly. Although reduction of growth is necessary for a change of policy, it will also make that change more difficult, especially if the reduction turns out to be relatively large. Indeed, it would force the state to limit its commitments and most importantly to turn to private companies. Considering that in many places relations between the administration and private business are corrupt, the decisions of the central government will largely be ignored: this is what is to be feared on the basis of the preliminary reports concerning the application of the law on labor contracts, a law that has been in force since

January 2008.[3] The central and provincial authorities will then confront a dilemma with regard to the pace of granting the social concessions that have sheltered countries that industrialized before China: on one side the threat of social disturbances, on the other the danger of the breakup of the coalition in power.

A path was worked out in the West, and one also may be found in China. In the recent past, management and labor have showed themselves to be more capable of pragmatism and compromise than had been expected. Analyzing workers' protests, Jean Louis Rocca has showed, for example, that the government was smarter and less violent than had been thought and that protesting workers were relatively pragmatic and moderate. But the result was one sided: state industries were abruptly purged and reorganized. In addition, this occurred in relatively limited local and regional situations. What would happen if the social problem was posed at the national level and if agitation in the major urban centers and their universities produced a proliferation of free unions, thereby presenting a political problem that is more truly national than in 1989, once again for the outside world to see?

Improbable Democracy

At this point in the argument, it might, of course, seem logical to appeal to democracy, and that is what many will do, in China and especially abroad. More representative institutions, a state more distinct from the communist party, free elections, and unions and the press freed from tyranny: part of the solution at least is probably to be found in this direction—although the concrete functioning of the Western democracies should induce some caution. These propositions will carry some weight.

Yet it is hard to imagine that they can provide a quick overall solution. Not that China is incapable for some "cultural" reasons of using the democratic model, that is, appropriating and reworking it. But we have to recall that it is enormously larger than Taiwan and controlled by a party that has been totalitarian and has done everything possible to eliminate the social seeds of pluralism, in circumstances favorable to it, whereas the democratic model is still partially discredited by its failure in 1989 and by the fact that the democratic model, in the words of Guy Hermet, has entered its winter around the world.

Furthermore, as I have noted earlier, the inevitable disturbances are more likely to lead to authoritarian solutions, perhaps close to those adopted in Russia and taking advantage of the model left behind by the Guomindang. It will probably take a long additional process for the democratic model to make substantial progress in China. This process will obviously involve important social transformations: living conditions and living standards that foster the individualization of life, improvement in education and information, a stronger and more active civil society.

China Confronts Its Fate

This does not mean that the worst will necessarily come out of the events that can be predicted. If the regime weakens in the face of difficulty and disorder, it will probably be encouraged at first to develop its policy of a "harmonious society." That would commit it to making more vigorous use of the notion of justice and perhaps to reducing even further the use of violence, important and significant signs of progress. But "communism" would remain in command, which would perhaps impede other developments. By contrast, more pronounced disturbances and an authoritarian resolution of the crisis would open more broadly—and perhaps also more dangerously—the horizon of the future.

However, whatever may occur, Chinese society will no longer be able to avoid confronting its fate with its own eyes. Under Mao, its fate was imposed on it, and its leaders treated it as subordinate. During the period opened by Deng Xiaoping, the Chinese were able to look at their fate, albeit through the glasses of the economic growth that had been imposed on them and that they wore willingly. Government and people are going to have to do without those glasses, or they will have to change. China will confront its fate, and the challenge will be to construct it.

Afterword

China Moves Toward a Consumer Economy

THIS BOOK WAS PUBLISHED IN FRANCE RIGHT AFTER THE 2008 Olympic Games, during the early stages of the developing financial crisis. Not only did the games yield unquestionable sporting successes, but they also displayed China's ability—later confirmed by the Universal Exposition of Shanghai from May to October 2010—to organize a very large-scale event and to bring the entire world to listen to the imperial discourse it now proclaims.

China Number Two

But the financial crisis is far more important. Beginning in the United States in September 2008, it seriously weakened the most developed economies in the world today: the United States, Europe, and Japan. Their rate of growth declined nearly to the point of stagnation, and the increasingly precarious financial condition of their governments has produced great turbulence in the financial markets.

On the other hand, the world crisis has brought out the comparatively much greater health of the Chinese economy. It was to some degree protected by the relative isolation of its financial markets and by its ability to control the information it received and gave out. The winter of 2008–2009 and the following spring were, of course, difficult for China, because orders and investments from the West fell, and many coastal factories had to close their doors. The rate of growth declined up to the summer of 2009, falling below 6 percent, but the authorities reacted by extending New Year vacations as long as possible and by helping many migrant workers to move back to their native villages.

Most important, they launched a massive stimulus program dealing with the most urgent matters—gigantic building projects, major public works—that favored both large government companies and the provinces of the west and center that possessed large reserves of manpower and raw materials. Overall, the central, provincial, and local authorities injected sums equivalent to 40 percent of GDP into the economy during the winter of 2008–2009. It is estimated that since then the Chinese money supply has been multiplied by 2.6 times.[1]

In doing so, the authorities in Beijing ignored the concerns of some economic experts who questioned the privileges granted to government companies, pointed out the danger of aggravating excess capacity, and noted the relative neglect of the green economy. One of them, Yu Yongding, close to Prime Minister Wen Jiabao, was bold enough to publish two articles in the *Financial Times*.[2] But it must be acknowledged that the effect of this stimulus was spectacular. The Chinese economy soon resumed its forward movement: GDP grew about 8 percent in 2009, 10.3 percent in 2010, and probably around 9 percent in 2011.[3] In the process, the Chinese economy has become the third largest in the world, behind the United States and the European Union, thanks to Japanese economic slowdown. In thirty years, its production has grown fifteen-fold. And four of the ten largest companies in the world are now Chinese.[4]

Many observers are still troubled by the risks incurred by the Beijing leadership. The annual inflation created by the sudden increase in liquidity has reached about 6 percent, and this has been particularly badly received by the population, because the price of pork (an essential ingredient in Chinese cuisine) has increased by more than 50 percent. Housing costs are also soaring: prices have tripled in the thirty-five largest cities over the last ten years.[5] In addition, excess investment prompted by the thirst for profits on the part of authorities at every level has placed the finances of many localities at risk. Their overall indebtedness is estimated at 25 percent of GNP, and some experts estimate that bad debts in the banking system amount to an even larger sum. The province of Hubei, for example, has published an investment program for the next five years of 1.8 trillion euros, or ten times its 2009 GDP.[6]

Rightly or wrongly, however, the majority of observers are still optimistic. This optimism seems justified in their eyes by the duration of Chinese growth—already three decades, which persuades conservative observers—as well as by the existence of significant reserves for development in the center and west of the country. According to this analysis, the global crisis has provided a further opportunity for lasting growth that might otherwise have slowed its pace. Not only is it lasting, but it influences the current world situation.

This is indeed the difference between the Chinese triumph and the equivalent earlier victories won by the Japanese, Taiwanese, and South Korean economies. It provides further resources for a country that is not small but large, a regime not modest but ambitious, and leaders who intend to use economic performance as an instrument of power. What is important about Chinese growth from 2008 to 2011 is that it has given the country the means to present itself as the real challenger to the American empire, in an economic competition that provides it with opportunities to progress even further.

The Chinese leaders are aware of economic and demographic arguments that suggest that the decline of the country's economic growth rate is inevitable, but they have followed a cardinal rule of political action: reap the benefits of the success that come your way, as you can always retreat later. This rule was especially imperative because, whatever the financial gluttony of their children and colleagues, their fundamental project was never anything but political, in direct continuity with Mao

Zedong. Today, as in the past, the goal is to raise China to the highest rank in the world, regardless of the moment, the occasion, or the means employed.

Times Change

But this triumph has done nothing to remedy the huge difficulties and changes that have been underway for the last few years. It is as though—at a rate of growth in any event much higher than that of Western countries—recent successes represented simultaneously the peak and the beginning of the end of an era, the era of China as a socially authoritarian export economy. The reason for this is that the same crisis that has weakened its rivals is also compelling China to change its mode of production, and this change will in itself decisively modify the organization of society and subsequently of political power. After having passed through the history of the modern production economy in a few decades, China is about to enter the age of the consumer economy, which will be much more complicated, at least for the regime.

The new times are already taking shape. The global crisis has reduced American orders. In addition, the European market is starting to become more difficult, because under the current circumstances the trade deficit is becoming increasingly burdensome. European administrations are growing harder to deal with (or are less distracted). For the first time, in the spring of 2011, Chinese exports were penalized because of government subsidies, and EU leaders have more frequently joined American protests against the undervaluation of the yuan.[7] It is, however, true that China enjoys close relations with German leaders, and it is especially true that Chinese investments will be increasingly sought after by Europe in crisis. Yet the glorious and untroubled era of Chinese exports is coming to an end.

China's extraordinary trade offensive is also continuing in the rest of the world, but it no longer has the same dynamism as in the past. The advantages of products "made in China" are well known, but their drawbacks are as well: often dubious quality, questionable trade practices, disregard of local legislation. In Africa, for example, Chinese interests have been firmly established, but illusions have been dispelled everywhere. Everyone knows that Chinese firms are working only to make the maximum profit. China is now a great power, with all the attendant advantages—and drawbacks. Everyone knows it is looking for raw materials and markets and that it competes profitably with Western interests, but everyone also understands that its enterprises are not systematically more advantageous than those of its competitors.

Behind this "normalization" of the Chinese image, another new feature is appearing: Chinese products are not so inexpensive. Indeed, rising production costs, already perceptible in recent years, have been confirmed. The most spectacular reason for this is the increase in wages, confirmed in 2009 and 2010—some sources indicate an annual rate higher than 10 percent since 2006.[8] This increase has been quickened by an increasingly observable phenomenon: the shortage of manpower, explained both by the coming to maturity of the generations born during the period of limitation of births and by the development of some rural zones, which are beginning to retain their young workers.[9] But more generally, all costs are increasing, both making the establishment of companies in China less advantageous and subjecting expatriates to ever higher wage and benefit costs. These increases have contributed to the relocation of many Chinese and foreign exporting firms to interior regions of China or to neighboring countries—or to increasingly automated production.[10]

The result is that although foreign trade remains strong and highly advantageous to Beijing, it has begun to lose its importance in the Chinese economy. Its contribution to growth is estimated to have declined by 3 percent in 2009. And the share of consumption in the economy has stopped its fall and stabilized at about 35 percent—a figure still comparatively weak.[11] Automobiles and tourism are among the most sharply growing sectors of consumption in cities, where many official commentators have detected the appearance of a middle stratum that now is said to include 230 million city dwellers.[12]

In addition, the real battle for the development of a consumer economy has been joined in two central areas. The first is that of social policies, which are alone able to stimulate a rapid growth of consumption: facing many difficulties, they are in the process of shifting from pilot programs to widespread adoption (although at still limited levels).[13] Added to this are measures designed to facilitate land swaps in the countryside, which, according to recent evidence, have fostered the revitalization of some rural zones.

The second battle is for the reform of the educational and health-care systems, as well as for launching programs for social housing, major conditions for the necessary reduction in the insanely high savings rate—about 45 percent—which the Chinese population has imposed on itself. In these three areas, the interests at stake are huge and enjoy protection at the upper levels of the ruling apparatus. The information available has not yet enabled us to measure developments, but clear signs point to the difficulties encountered: for example, the intensity of the central government's efforts to persuade local authorities to launch building programs, the growing number of rich Chinese who seek medical care abroad, and the spectacular increase in many school fees and university tuition charges.

Other long-range developments are underway that are making the organization of a different economy and society inevitable. Some are demographic in nature. For example, the population is aging: those over sixty now comprise 12 percent of the population; that will rise to 17 percent in 2020 and 23.4 percent in 2030.[14] Other developments are social. Urbanization is accelerating: China has 220 cities with more than a million inhabitants, and gigantic megalopolises are taking shape around Beijing-Tianjin and Guangdong. It will therefore be necessary to organize ways of living together in these new urban settings, whose dangers and requirements the regime is just now discovering.[15] Social psychology is also developing at astonishing speed. Living longer but suffering ever more from solitude, without sufficient resources to pay for leisure activities, older people are beginning to form a problem category. The young are also rapidly changing: members of a one-child generation, they are less hard working, greater consumers, and drawn to new forms of leisure activities, partly inspired by foreign countries or in connection with them; forty million of them play the piano, and study in the West is highly prized.[16] Although they still ask their parents' consent to get married, they divorce much more, nearly one out of five—usually for financial reasons.[17]

Jealousy and Inequality

The wound affecting contemporary Chinese society more than any other is still inequality, the universal recognition of which has produced in public opinion an anger that has obscured the very real progress recorded in almost everyone's living standards. Added to the hatred and contempt provoked by a corrupt ruling class, this feeling explains why the regime that excites admiration or fear throughout the world inspires anxiety or anger in most of China's inhabitants. Among them, the wish to go abroad has declined only marginally: only one person returns to China for every three who leave. But it is now the rich who are leaving, to enjoy greater security or Western health-care systems.

Overall, then, social jealousy has only gotten worse since the global crisis began, particularly during the hard winter of 2008–2009. Chinese society is in fact still divided into castes and classes and is driven by a twofold movement of social mobility and defense, and, thanks to the Internet and television, castes and classes have more and more information about one another. Moreover, these inequalities are still based on the same yardstick: money, which is more than ever the supreme social value, so much so that it often rules feelings. A female contestant on a TV dating show said, "I'd rather cry in a BMW than laugh on a bicycle"; another young woman turned down a date with a man who did not own an apartment, saying, "Without an apartment, love isn't possible."[18] Periodically, the society laments the excesses that constantly recur: for example, in October 2011, a truck driver decided to run over a child he had just hit in order to avoid hospitalization costs.[19] Then questions abound in the press and on the Internet.

But social differentiation is at work, and every stratum of society poses particular problems. At the top, the rich are subject to both admiration and jealousy, or even contempt. They have never been so numerous: There were 1.6 million millionaires in 2009, and there will probably be more than four million by 2015. Among them are 130 U.S. dollar billionaires, and although only one-third of them are Chinese Communist Party members, they all are armed with political protection and no longer intimidated by the global jet set: attending the Bal des Débutantes in November 2009, one of the high points of the social season in Paris, were two young Chinese women, one of whom was the granddaughter of Jia Qinglin, a high dignitary of the CCP.[20] Rich Chinese are even increasingly internationalized, to the extent that some change their citizenship and transfer the bulk of their fortune abroad, often to the United States and Canada.

At the core of urban society are found a series of intermediate strata that are doing their utmost to help their children succeed in the crucially important race for diplomas, internships, and good jobs. They at least are expecting a good deal from the future, are interested in foreign matters, and are apparently more aware of the authorities' great national plan—and they will not forgive failure.

The huge peasantry—still about six hundred million people—is both the great mute figure in the country and the major obstacle to democratization in the view of city dwellers, because they wonder to what extremes the peasantry might draw the rest of the electorate. The regime's program is ambiguous but enables it to avoid troubles: it is to draw the best peasant children to cities but also to revive the best-endowed and closest rural areas. In ordinary times, the peasantry has allowed itself to grow weak and change, but trouble is brewing. Villages are the sites of most of the incidents that worry the sociologists of the Central Committee, and religious sects are proliferating in the overpopulated plains of central China.

At the top of rural society but at the bottom of city society are the 170 million migrants from the countryside, discriminated against but hard working. They are increasingly considered by the enlightened fraction of the government as future consumers and as less and less disciplined.[21] Much more turbulent than their elders, young migrants are a barometer of social discipline. When the economy is doing well, they remain collectively disciplined, although they are individually more demanding. But as soon as slowdowns occur, strikes proliferate.

The Political Challenge

In a shifting and complicated social situation, the magnitude of the tasks facing Chinese decision makers is enormous. First and foremost, they have to respond to the inevitable reduction of the role of foreign trade in outlining social policies for the transition to a consumer economy. But that will not be all. They will also have to introduce more equity into society to make life more livable.

These major tasks will be the responsibility of the new political leadership that the Eighteenth Party Congress will elect in October 2012. At that point, a process of gradual replacement will begin, which is wise in principle but conducive to conflict. It must be acknowledged that the decade just ending was as a whole very positive. After a rather difficult initial period, President Hu Jintao and Prime Minister Wen Jiabao succeeded rather remarkably on the whole. They were able to take advice from the best experts and especially to make decisions by basing their authority on a majority of the Central Committee. To accomplish this, they took into account the two principal factions, representing coastal China (primarily interested in foreign trade) and interior China (more favorable to reform and economic reorientation), as well as a "center group" made up of the fifty members of the Central Committee who are "sons of princes," respected and influential descendants of the companions of Mao Zedong.

Hence, priority was at first given to economic stimulus in 2008–2009, later shifting to social policies and the development of the Chinese west. Over time, Wen Jiabao, the highly reformist prime minister, lost influence to the benefit of President Hu Jintao, who might be tempted, like Jiang Zemin ten years earlier, to extend slightly the period of his domination: this is one of the first problems that will be posed.

The succession has been intelligently engineered for several years, and the probable successors, Xi Jinping and Li Keqiang, seem well chosen. Both have solid experience as provincial leaders and are considered sturdy characters, perhaps even stronger that those of their predecessors. Xi Jinping has a particularly singular biography, both in his personal choices—he climbed through almost every position from the lowest, and his second wife is a singer—and in his ancestry—he is the son of a high-quality leader whom Mao dismissed early on and who later came out in favor of the May 1989 demonstrations—as well as in his obvious connections with other "sons of princes," particularly the remarkable Bo Xilai, the boss of Chongqing, and some military commanders, such as Liu Yuan, the son of Liu Shaoqi.[22] Li Keqiang, for his part, is fairly popular among provincial leaders of the interior—for better or worse, because he was implicated in the contaminated-blood scandal in Henan in the 1990s.

These two leaders, who should be supported by several other newly elected officials, thus have going for them substantial experience and many connections in the party and the army. Another advantage is at the same time a drawback: they are typical products of the apparatus, and they have been living for decades in a closed milieu and, more recently, in luxury. It might be thought that they have the qualities needed to maneuver between factions and even to impose truces and compromises on them. If they are able to cooperate, they can take advantage of the fact that Xi Jinping is especially powerful in Shanghai and the coastal provinces and Li Keqiang is likewise in the interior provinces.

But what they lack, aside from regular association with ordinary people, is a real political culture, international experience, and especially a program responding clearly to the two necessities of the hour: the transition to a consumer economy and an answer to the emerging major social problems. And that is not all. It is highly possible that new dangers will arise from Chinese and global economic circumstances as well as from the extraordinary fragility of the sociopolitical fabric of China. The real question in that case is whether the two new leaders will be able to rise above the immediate situation and the interests of their caste to respond coherently to the major problems they will encounter.

Anxiety Persists

The singularity of the situation is that there is no possible line of development for China that is devoid of danger. This is obvious with respect to economic matters. If Beijing delays encouraging the transition to a consumer economy, weaknesses of every variety will surface, because such a transition is inevitable. For example, one dare not imagine the effect on China of a real slump in the world economy: it would simply be a catastrophe for more than 1.3 billion human beings. But if the transition occurs under stable global conditions, it will certainly give rise to a series of positive developments for the country, developments that will, however, be dangerous for the authorities and thereby for the equilibrium of the system. This is what explains the extreme caution of the Beijing government as well as the disagreements among factions.

The domination of the CCP over the population fits very well with the rather simple arrangement of an economy of production and export based on massive investments. In this tightly controlled economy, large factories contribute to the domination of social space, production models call for little change, production plans are rigorous and lasting, channels of command are clear, discipline is stable, and administrative controls and financial levies of all kinds remain relatively easy.

The consumer economy already established in major Chinese cities has only begun to modify this pattern. The more widespread it becomes—with inevitable limits and delays in the countryside—the higher its political cost will be. Indeed, from every point of view it will be harder to control because of the constant variation of clientele, models, sites and units of production, and inevitably of financial yields and means of control and taxation. In particular, but not only, in luxury goods, the distinction between foreign tastes and the real or supposed tastes of the Chinese clientele will be much harder to maintain. In a word, the new economy will be less directed and predictable, more random, more disconnected from the political sphere, and less rigorously "national," especially because tourism will expand further in both directions between China and the world. Depending more on client taste and choice, the economy will also produce less guaranteed and more variable financial results.

There is certainly no doubt that the authorities will strive to compensate for these new difficulties by using their classic but nonetheless powerful means of control of financial and communications circuits. Even so, although not transforming anything all at once, the advent of the consumer economy will reinforce developments already in progress: the difficulty of controlling an increasingly complex economic universe and the influences of all kinds coming from abroad, and especially the widening of the individual sphere.

A More Politicized Domestic Scene?

These developments obviously look positive to the eyes of a Western public, but in the Chinese context they carry complications and provoke anxiety. First and foremost, this is because the transition to a consumer economy and the other social and demographic changes will produce a decrease and especially a greater variability of the rate of growth. And if there is one demand that its mistrust of the government keeps the population from abandoning, it is the demand for a very rapid, regular, and predictable rise in living standards. It is therefore not hard to foresee that the transition to a consumer economy will add to already known factors—the widening of individual liberties and opportunities to travel, the widespread use of the Internet—to make the relations between the government (or, rather, governments) and the population (or, rather, populations) more difficult and even dangerous.

This point is worth describing more fully. In this situation, the regime is paradoxically a victim of the prohibition of politics it has imposed on its components and the population both to avoid having to justify and discipline itself and to prevent any organized opposition. This prohibition—supported by the compartmentalization of all propaganda, administrative, and party organs—has had the effect of transforming the loose grouping of party and state into a multiplicity of cells. These cells each operate for themselves and foster at local levels forms of uncontrolled authoritarianism that give way only in the face of popular revolt or violence from superior authorities.

In these circumstances, political opposition is impossible and even unthinkable, because—and this is what is of the greatest interest to the leadership—there can be no general protest, only local agitation against any particular excess of a minor local potentate: the seizure of "illegal" children to be sold to traffickers, a factory poisoning the atmosphere, a building program causing excessive evictions, a road or railroad going through a village without compensation for the inhabitants, and so on. In such situations, the attitude of local authorities and their superiors is not necessarily repressive; it depends largely on the balance of power, for example, the connections of local despots and their ability to hush up their abuses. A number of communities in revolt are simply crushed, whereas, close to major cities, sorts of "Gallic villages" have been able to negotiate land use and even to continue to resist publicly—this is often the case near airports.

But the problem (and the sociologists on the Central Committee are rightly concerned about this) is that there is hardly any locality that has not at one time or another been affected by collective discontent or even agitation. This explains a characteristic of Chinese society that surprises many Western travelers: there are few Chinese who speak the language of opposition, but there are also few who like or respect their cadres or their leaders.

The whole problem is to avoid having this dislike spread beyond any particular locality and therefore become politicized, avoid a circumstance in which the entire Chinese population would be moved by the same serious dissatisfaction with the authorities, whether because of a limitation of its freedom or a diminution or threat to its rising living standards. Developments in the area of individual freedom have been and remain generally positive, so it is the development of the economy that is now the focus of attention. There is nothing new in this: for the last thirty years, the Chinese population has worried about the future. The reason for this is that it despises—often wrongly—national and provincial leaders whom it imagines to be as greedy and incompetent as the local cadres it knows too well: this is another drawback to the depoliticization brought about by localization. In addition, over time the population has become familiar with the mechanisms of the capitalist economy, including the stock market: many families in major cities have one member devoted almost professionally to the stock market. These individuals are well aware that a decline of the Chinese economic growth rate is probable, and they are watching for advance warnings. Some of them were the first to inform me of the general increase in production costs in China at a time (the middle of the 2000s), when it was generally unknown. But, of course, few of them will agree to pay the price of an inevitable development without vigorous protest.

It is therefore not very risky to predict that the inevitable entry of China into a consumer economy will mark the beginning of a shift from localism and a politicization of relations between a population often unified in protest and a government held responsible for greater uncertainty about rising living standards. It is also likely that particular factors will sharpen discontent: habits of corruption and conspicuous consumption among the plutobureaucratic class in power, the complete lack of real civic education, and above all the fact that half the huge Chinese population is still living in scarcity and more than one hundred million in poverty.

Greater Foreign Presence in China

I have already pointed out that the transition to a consumer economy will further erode the barrier between China and the rest of the world. Through fashion, tourism, culture, and cuisine, the outside world will become increasingly present and better known. Its attraction will probably be different from what it was during Deng Xiaoping's first decade in power, probably less intense and naïve and hence more critical with regard to both foreign countries and to China itself. The regime's propaganda will no longer be able to rely on arguments from authority to respond to the lure of the outside world. But it will also find new arguments in the difficulties encountered by the old democracies of the West, especially if it also further reduces the surviving traces of Marxist-Leninist ideology in its language and continues its evolution toward a proud nationalism and an apparently Confucian moralism. Both might simultaneously counterbalance and mask a liberation of social behavior in part colored by the West.

In essential areas, however, painful choices will probably be hard to avoid. In politics, the China-centered pride and nationalistic vanity awakened by recent Chinese successes will be more difficult to maintain once societies are also compared to one another in terms of their levels of social protection, their leisure activities, and their cultural policies.

The national "arrogance" that the Chinese public is currently so taken with could give way to other appetites: culture, pleasure, happiness.

If China does manage to construct a consumer economy and a consumer society, it will be unable to avoid moving toward a more or less complete reversal of its political and moral priorities. From the end of the Opium Wars to the present day, it has consistently defined itself by its comparative degree of power. Because that definition has now become positive and because consumerism has made its appearance, a new goal has become possible, a kind of "social happiness."

It is clear that if this development is confirmed, it should eventually compel a decline of the authoritarianism that governs Chinese politics and society. But it is possible to wonder whether an already crumbling pillar of that authoritarianism will not be even further weakened beforehand: the subjection of Chinese women is likely to be the second victim of the consumer economy. By importing images and concepts from abroad, particularly from the West, the new economy will give more importance to Chinese women. It will establish a private life where women play a less subordinate role at the center of the definition of needs and desires. It will reduce, without necessarily making them disappear entirely, the "niches" where "virile" energy takes refuge and where "struggle" (between classes or nations) persists. It will reduce the place occupied by politics and sooner or later will force the CCP to appoint at least one woman to the Permanent Committee of the Politburo.

Overall, then, one may be optimistic about many of the long-term effects of the consumer economy toward which China has been forced to move, because these effects are likely to weaken the political and social forms of the authoritarianism that prevails in the country. But that authoritarianism will be forcefully supported by the political regime and the vast interests it protects. In the early stages, at least, the decline of the production economy is likely to foster the appearance of even more widespread social disturbances and interregional tensions, for in a world more subject to chance and a history less written in advance, the issue of national unity could also be reopened. In short, the spread of the consumer society is likely to force China finally to reinvent itself. The most urgent and difficult unknown is how quickly that will occur.

Abbreviations

AFP	Agence France Presse
ALC	*Aujourd'hui la Chine*
CD	*China Daily*
CQ	*China Quarterly*
FT	*Financial Times*
IHT	*International Herald Tribune*
L	*Libération*
LC	*La Croix*
LE	*Les Échos*
LF	*Le Figaro*
LM	*Le Monde*
LP	*Le Parisien*
NW	*The Nikkei Weekly*
NYT	*New York Times*
SCMP	*South China Morning Post*
TE	*The Economist*
WSJ	*Wall Street Journal*

Notes

Introduction: The New "Chinese Moment"

1. LP, September 24, 2006; IHT, May 10, 2005.
2. LM, November 20, 2007.
3. Gilbert Étienne, *Chine-Inde, la grande competition* (Paris: Dunod, 2007), 86; AFP, Beijing, October 25, 2007.
4. Philippe Cohen and Luc Richard, *La Chine sera-t-elle notre cauchemar?* (Paris: Mille et une nuits, 2005), 9.
5. Lucien Bianco, *Les origines de la révolution chinoise, 1915–1945* (Paris: Gallimard, 2007), 348.
6. Benoît Vermander calculates that if China's consumption level reached that of Taiwan it would need 40 million barrels a year, whereas annual world production is now only 85 million barrels. See Vermander, *Chine brune ou Chine verte?* (Paris: Presses de Sciences Po, 2007), 55.
7. AFP, Beijing, December 5, 2007.
8. Susan Shirk *China, Fragile Superpower* (New York: Oxford University Press, 2007), 9.

9. I presented my investigations and encounters in *Comprendre la Chine d'aujourd'hui* (Paris: Perrin, 2007).

Book I. Measure for Measure: Introduction

1. Marie Holzman and Bernard Debord, *Wei Jingsheng, un chinois inflexible* (Paris: Bleu de Chine, 2005), 301.

2. Lucien Bianco, *Les origines de la révolution chinoise, 1915–1945* (Paris: Gallimard, 2007), 405.

1. The Regime's New Foundations

1. Minxin Pei, *China's Trapped Transition: The Limits of Developmental Autocracy* (Cambridge, Mass.: Harvard University Press, 2006), 26.

2. Ibid., 81.

3. Jean-Pierre Cabestan et al., "Le renouveau des professions judiciaires en Chine," in *La Chine et la démocratie*, ed. Mireille Delmas-Marty and Pierre-Étienne Will (Paris: Fayard, 2007), 683.

4. See Stéphanie Balme, "Judiciarisation du politique et politisation du juridique dans la Chine des réformes," in *La Chine et la démocratie*, ed. Mireille Delmas-Marty and Pierre-Étienne Will (Paris: Fayard, 2007), 577–613. For a specific example of a verdict against the police, see WSJ, April 30, 2006; see also IHT, June 1, 2007.

5. Sina.com, July 5, 2007.

6. SCMP, September 4, 2007; AFP, Beijing, November 26, 2007.

7. On the "public" market in organs in contemporary China, see LM, August 18, 2006. A kidney transplant requires a wait of only two weeks.

8. TE, September 6, 2003.

9. It is very well analyzed in Isabelle Attané, *Une Chine sans femmes* (Paris: Perrin, 2004).

10. On the treatment of female workers, see Pun Ngai, *Made in China: Women Factory Workers in a Global Workplace* (Durham, N.C.: Duke University Press, 2005).

11. CD, December 29, 2005; *Xinjingbao* [Beijing News], December 14, 2007.

12. WSJ, August 30, 2006.

13. IHT, June 25, 2007.

14. *Xinjingbao*, August 26, 2006.

15. They are admirably captured in the journal *Lao Zhaopian* [Old Photographs], which can be found in all good Chinese bookstores.

16. Frédéric Bobin, *Good Bye Mao?* (Paris: La Martinière, 2006), 128; Pierre Haski, *Le sang de la Chine* (Paris: Grasset, 2005), 128.

17. AFP, Beijing, January 27, 2008.

18. Susan Shirk, *China, Fragile Superpower* (New York: Oxford University Press, 2007), 92; AFP, October 19, 2007.

19. LM, September 20, 2006; see also Pierre Haski, *Internet et la Chine* (Paris: Seuil, 2008).

20. *Aujourd'hui la Chine*, November 27, 2007.

21. Quoted by Valérie Niquet in her roundup of the Congress for IFRI; see ifri .org.

22. LE, August 31, 2007; LM, September 20, 2006.

23. Willy Wo-Lap Lam, *Chinese Politics in the Hu Jintao Era* (Armonk, N.Y.: M. E. Sharpe, 2006), 230.

24. And residents of Shenzhen succeeded in getting the cancellation of a planned expressway. See IHT, December 18, 2007; see also AFP, Beijing, January 21, 2008.

25. *Zhongguo qingnianbao* [China Youth Daily], August 21, 2006; *Beijing qingnianbao* [Beijing Youth Daily], July 10, 2006.

26. Sohu.com, June 25, 2007; IHT, September 13, 2005.

27. Benoît Vermander, *Chine brune ou Chine verte?* (Paris: Presses de Sciences Po, 2007), 141.

28. See below, book 3, chapter 6.

29. I closely analyzed this degeneration of the totalitarian control system in my book on the Chinese gulag. See Jean-Luc Domenach, *Chine, l'archipel oublié* (Paris: Fayard, 1992).

30. François Gipouloux, *La Chine du XXIe siècle: Une nouvelle super-puissance?* (Paris: Armand Colin, 2006), 13; Bobin, *Good Bye Mao?*, 235. According to Lam, *Chinese Politics in the Hu Jintao Era*, 141, one-third of district governments are bankrupt. On this point, see also IHT, September 19, 2002.

31. Guy Sorman, *The Empire of Lies: The Truth About China in the Early Twenty-First Century*, trans. Asha Puri (New York: Encounter Books, 2008), 76.

32. Pei, *China's Trapped Transition*, 144ff. He goes on to say, less convincingly, that the Chinese state is a "decentralized predatory state." Bobin, *Good Bye Mao?*, 176, evokes the "stifling effect of microclimates."

33. IHT, February 15, 2007.

34. For example, Maria Edi, although she judges that in the "important" areas local officials are generally loyal. See her "State Capacity and Local Agent Control in China: CCP Cadre Management from a Township Perspective," *CQ* 173 (2003): 35–52.

35. Jean-Luc Domenach, *Aux origines du Grand Bond en avant, le cas d'une province chinoise* (Paris: Presses de la FNSP, 1982), 75ff.

36. See David S. G. Goodman, "Structuring Local Identity: Nation, Province, and County in Shanxi During the 1990s," *CQ* 172 (2002), 837–862.

37. See below.

38. Personal information.

39. Lam, *Chinese Politics in the Hu Jintao Era*, 113.

40. Maurice Agulhon, *The Republic in the Village: The People of the Var from the French Revolution to the Second Republic*, trans. Janet Lloyd (Cambridge: Cambridge University Press, 1982). On village elections in China, see the contribution by Gunter Schubert to Mireille Delmas-Marty and Pierre-Étienne Will, *La Chine et la démocratie* (Paris: Fayard, 2007), 713ff.; Pei, *China's Trapped Transition*, 72ff.; and Jean-Louis Rocca, *La condition chinoise* (Paris: Karthala, 2006), 259ff.

41. LC, August 22, 2007.

42. IHT, February 14, 2007.

43. Pei, *China's Trapped Transition*, 92.

44. For a concrete example, see the account by Bastien Affeltranger, "Haut voltage, haute voltige: Les ONG chinoises face aux barrages du Yunnan," *Monde chinois* 2, no. 1 (Winter 2005). See also Guobin Yang, "Environmental NGOs and Institutional Dynamics in China," *CQ* 181 (2005): 46–66.

45. *Aujourd'hui la Chine*, January 22, 2008.

46. TE, August 18, 2007.

47. Yongshun Cai, "Collective Ownership or Cadres Ownership? The Non-Agricultural Use of Farmland in China," *CQ* 175 (2003): 662–80.

48. Kevin O'Brien and Lianjiang Li, *Rightful Resistance in Rural China* (Cambridge: Cambridge University Press, 2006).

49. Information presented at the Shanghai Academy of Social Sciences in February 2006 and in the *China Economic Times*, June 6, 2006.

50. LM, October 19, 2007; January 17, 2008.

51. LM, November 6, 2002; Erik Izraëlewicz, *Quand la Chine change le monde* (Paris: Grasset, 2005), 270; Lam, *Chinese Politics in the Hu Jintao Era*, 39; *Xinjingbao* (Beijing News), February 7, 2006; *Xingdao Ribao* [Sing Tao Daily], October 16, 2006.

52. LE, June 19, 2007; Gilles Guiheux, "Les nouvelles classes sociales chinoises: Comment penser les inégalités?" in *Asie, entre pragmatisme et attentisme*, ed. Sophie Boisseau du Rocher and François Godement (Paris: La Documentation française, 2006), 24; lecture by Jean-Louis Rocca at CERI, Paris, January 20, 2008.

53. TE, March 11, 2006.

54. See the afterword to this book.

55. Bobin, *Good Bye Mao?*, 237.

56. Lucien Bianco, *Les origines de la révolution chinoise, 1915–1945* (Paris: Gallimard, 2007), 410.

57. Marie-Claire Bergère, *Capitalisme et capitalistes en Chine* (Paris: Perrin, 2007).

58. Frédéric Koller, *Portraits de Chine* (Paris: Alvik, 2004), 172. See also Pei, *China's Trapped Transition*, 93, 154; FT, May 10, 2005. It is noteworthy that Miao Yu, the mayor of Wuhan, is the former general manager of the Dongfeng Motor Corporation.

59. Bobin, *Good Bye Mao?*, 97ff., 115ff.

60. As I have shown elsewhere, taking inspiration from the work of Yves Chevrier. See Jean-Luc Domenach, *Où va la Chine?* (Paris: Fayard, 2002), 327–330.

61. Bianco, *Les origines de la révolution chinoise, 1915–1945*, 360.

2. In a New World

1. SCMP, July 19, 2002.

2. Huang Yasheng, *Selling China: Direct Investments During the Reform Era* (Cambridge: Cambridge University Press, 2003).

3. LM, December 15, 2007.

4. CD, July 10, 2007.

5. Personal notes. See also FT, April 12, 2007.

6. Personal notes; CD, March 19, 2007.

3. The Magnitude and Weaknesses of Growth

1. Quoted in Erik Izraëlewicz, *Quand la Chine change le monde* (Paris: Grasset, 2005), 12.

2. AFP Beijing, December 22, 2007.

3. Benoît Vermander, *Chine brune ou Chine verte?* (Paris: Presses de Sciences Po, 2007), 70; LM, September 4, 2007; FT, September 16, 2006.

4. Barry Naughton, *The Chinese Economy: Transitions and Growth* (Cambridge, Mass.: MIT Press, 2006); Izraëlewicz, *Quand la Chine change le monde*; François Gipouloux, *La Chine du XXIe siècle: Une nouvelle super-puissance?* (Paris: Armand Colin, 2006); TE, October 28, 2006; TE, March 31, 2007; LE, November 12, 2007; FT, April 17, 2007; SCMP, January 12, 2008; LE, January 14, 2008.

5. IHT, October 27–28, 2007.

6. Boris Cambreleng, *Faut-il avoir peur de la Chine?* (Toulouse: Milan, 2006), 26; Philippe Cohen and Luc Richard, *La Chine sera-t-elle notre cauchemar?* (Paris: Mille et une nuits, 2005), 205.

7. LM, August 14, 2007; IHT, November 2, 2007.

8. Izraëlewicz, *Quand la Chine change le monde*, 39.

9. *Alternatives internationales*, November 2006, 59; LM, July 10, 2007.

10. Izraëlewicz, *Quand la Chine change le monde*, 152; Thierry Wolton, *Le grand bluff chinois* (Paris: Laffont, 2007), 159ff.; IHT June 24–25, 2006; FT, January 14, 2007.

11. Gilbert Étienne, *Chine-Inde, la grande compétition* (Paris: Dunod, 2007), 149–150; Vermander, *Chine brune ou Chine verte?*, 58ff.; LM, July 10, 2007.

12. SCMP, May 4, 2007.

13. Vermander, *Chine brune ou Chine verte?*, 137; NW, October 22, 2007.

14. Yanqi Tong, "Bureaucracy Meets the Environment: Elite Perceptions in Six Chinese Cities," CQ 189 (March 2007): 100–121.

15. Izraëlewicz, *Quand la Chine change le monde*, 265; Frédéric Bobin, *Good Bye Mao?* (Paris: La Martinière, 2006), 195–196; LM, July 25, 2006; FT, August 23, 2006; NW, October 9, 2006; LM, July 18 and 21–22, 2007.

16. According to Bobin, *Good Bye Mao?*, 143. A report by Minxin Pei for the Carnegie Endowment estimates corruption at 3 percent of GDP but 10 percent of public expenditure, LE, October 16, 2007.

17. Sorman, *The Empire of Lies: The Truth About China in the Early Twenty-First Century*, trans. Asha Puri (New York: Encounter Books, 2008), 74.

18. Gipouloux, *La Chine du XXIe siècle*.

19. Sorman, *The Empire of Lies*, 78–79.

20. Gipouloux, *La Chine du XXIe siècle*; FT, September 17–18 and 25, 2006; LP, December 20, 2006.

21. Izraëlewicz, *Quand la Chine change le monde*, 52; Minxin Pei, *China's Trapped Transition: The Limits of Developmental Autocracy* (Cambridge, Mass.: Harvard University Press, 2006), 118ff; Wolton, *Le grand bluff chinois*, 116; Bobin, *Good Bye Mao?*, 200ff.

22. LM, April 15, May 31, and June 6, 2007.

23. FT, May 10, 2007; LE, October 15, 2007; AFP, November 7, 2007; LE, November 12, 2007.

24. FT, February 12, 2007.

25. IHT, April 18, 2007.

26. SCMP, February 1, 2008.

4. Explanation

1. FT, January 28, 2008.

2. Gilbert Étienne, *Chine-Inde, la grande compétition* (Paris: Dunod, 2007), 83.

3. FT, May 18, 2007. $5 billion was to go to the Congo, guaranteed by that country's mineral resources, thereby freeing it from a possible IMF loan.

4. Of the $300 million compensation that the Sudanese government pledged to the devastated Darfur region, $200 million came from a Chinese loan. FT, August 30, 2007.

5. Jean-Marc and Ydir Plantade, *La face cachée de la Chine* (Paris: Bourrin, 2006), 74; LF, December 6, 2006; TE, July 29, 2007.

6. NW, November 6, 2006.

7. WSJ, December 12, 2007.

8. Erik Izraëlewicz, *Quand la Chine change le monde* (Paris: Grasset, 2005), 87.

9. SCMP, January 24, 2008; IHT, April 4, 2005, April 3, 2006.

10. Personal notes; NW, September 4, 2006.

11. NW, December 18, 2006.

12. For example, on September 19, 2007, *Ouest-France* quoted French investors for whom Chinese wages had tripled between 1990 and 2005.

13. AFP, October 8, 2007; IHT, February 1, 2008.

14. *Zhongguo Qingnianbao* (China Youth Daily), November 18, 2005.

15. Personal notes, spring 2006.

16. Jean-Louis Rocca, *La condition chinoise* (Paris: Karthala, 2006), 119ff.

17. Frédéric Koller, *Portraits de Chine* (Paris: Alvik, 2004), 29.

18. Willy Wo-Lap Lam, *Chinese Politics in the Hu Jintao Era* (Armonk, N.Y.: M. E. Sharpe, 2006), 91.

19. *Zhongguo Qingnianbao*, December 6, 2005.

20. Frédéric Bobin, *Good Bye Mao?* (Paris: La Martinière, 2006), 227; Boris Cambreleng, *Faut-il avoir peur de la Chine?* (Toulouse: Milan, 2006), 42; social service of the French embassy, June 2006.

21. Isabelle Attané, *Une Chine sans femmes* (Paris: Perrin, 2004); IHT, June 29, 2006, March 21, 2007.

22. LM, February 8, 2006; FT, October 25. 2006; *Oriental Outlook*, May 26, 2005; Pierre Haski, *Le sang de la Chine* (Paris: Grasset, 2005), 197.

23. Benoît Vermander, *Chine brune ou Chine verte?* (Paris: Presses de Sciences Po, 2007), 86.

24. *Xinjingbao* (Beijing News), January 9, 2006; IHT, August 31-September 1, 2002; Haski, *Le sang de la Chine*, 195; Pierre Haski, *Le journal de Ma Yan* (Paris: Ramsay, 2002), 24.

25. For a specific example, see Jean-Luc Domenach, *Comprendre la Chine d'aujourd'hui* (Paris: Perrin, 2007), 167–68.

26. WSJ, May 6, 2003; IHT, August 20, 2005. According to sina.com (January 7, 2008), life expectancy has increased a little since 2005, reaching seventy-three in 2007.

27. LF, June 8, 2007, October 8, 2007.

28. New China News Agency, October 12, 2006; Wo-Lap Lam, *Chinese Politics in the Hu Jintao Era*, 68ff.

29. Wo-Lap Lam, *Chinese Politics in the Hu Jintao Era*, 41.

30. IHT, July 31, 2006.

31. Thierry Pairault, "Formation initiale et développement économique," *Perspectives chinoises* 65 (2001): 5–16.

32. IHT, August 6, 2006; *La vie des idées*, February 2006, 43ff.; TE, August 18, 2007.

33. Izraëlewicz, *Quand la Chine change le monde*, 208.

34. SCMP, May 4, 2007.

35. Personal notes; Aurore Merle and Michael Sztanke, *Étudiants chinois: Qui sont les élites de demain?* (Paris: Autrement, 2006); *Renmin Ribao* (People's Daily), July 5, 2006; AFP, August 17, 2006.

36. Susan Shirk, *China, Fragile Superpower* (New York: Oxford University Press, 2007), 17.

37. Personal notes of a stay of five years at Qinghua, which is ranked at the highest level of Chinese universities; FT, January 5 and 15, 2007; LM, October 12, 2007.

38. Étienne, *Chine-Inde, la grande compétition*, 188.

39. Guy Sorman, *The Empire of Lies: The Truth About China in the Early Twenty-First Century*, trans. Asha Puri (New York: Encounter Books, 2008), 107.

40. See Diana Hochraich, *Pourquoi l'Inde et la Chine ne domineront pas le monde de demain* (Paris: Ellipses, 2007), for a critique of Indian and Chinese growth.

41. François Gipouloux, *La Chine du XXIe siècle: Une nouvelle super-puissance?* (Paris: Armand Colin, 2006), 45.

42. AFP, Beijing, September 18, 2007; WSJ, January 13, 2008; SCMP, January 15, 2008.

43. LF, January 25, 2008; SCMP, January 29, 2008; LE, February 5, 2008; FT, February 4, 2008.

44. FT, September 11 and 12, 2007; SCMP September 12, 2007.

45. LM, December 11, 2007.

5. The Acceleration of History

1. Jean-Louis Rocca, *La condition chinoise* (Paris: Karthala, 2006).

2. Ibid.

3. AFP, Beijing, September 18, 2007.

4. WSJ, January 21, 2008.

5. Jean-Marc and Ydir Plantade, *La face cachée de la Chine* (Paris: Bourrin, 2006), confirm this estimate.

6. AFP, Beijing, October 8, 2007.

7. Philippe Richer, *La longue marche de la Chine en Afrique, 1504–2008* (Paris: Karthala, 2008), 47.

8. FT, January 21, 2008.

9. Susan Shirk, *China, Fragile Superpower* (New York: Oxford University Press, 2007), 53.

10. Marie-Claire Bergère, *Capitalisme et capitalistes en Chine* (Paris: Perrin, 2007), 250.

11. Benoît Vermander, *Chine brune ou Chine verte?* (Paris: Presses de Sciences Po, 2007), 95.

12. See the remarkable historical chronicle by Cheng Yingxiang and Claude Cadart, *Dégel de l'intelligence en Chine, 1976–1989* (Paris: Gallimard, 2004).

13. After these lines were written, *Le Figaro* published on January 7, 2008, an interesting article by Thierry Wolton suggesting that President Putin is following the "Chinese model." The hypothesis makes sense and is worth following up, but all the same I think that so far it is Beijing that has been following Moscow, more substantially and up to a more recent date than is often believed. On this issue see Jean-Luc Domenach, "Pékin pas si loin de Moscou!" in *Entre Kant et Kosovo*, ed. Anne-Marie Le Gloannec and Aleksander Smolar, 285–294 (Paris: Presses de Sciences Po, 2003).

6. Can China Be Governed?

1. Leila Choukroune, *La Chine et le maintien de la paix et de la sécurité internationale* (Paris: L'Harmattan, 1999), 628ff.

2. Andrew C. Mertha, "China's 'Soft' Centralization: Shifting Tiao/Kuai Authority Relations," *CQ* 184 (2005): 791–810.

3. Kai-yuan Tsui and Youqing Wang, "Between Separate Stoves and a Single Menu: Fiscal Decentralization in China," *CQ* 177 (2004): 71–90.

4. Huang Yasheng, *Selling China: Foreign Direct Investments During the Reform Era* (Cambridge: Cambridge University Press, 2003); Barry Naughton and Dali Yang, eds., *Holding China Together: Diversity and National Integration in the Post-Deng Era* (Cambridge: Cambridge University Press, 2004); Yunmin Sheng, "Central-Provincial Relations at the CCP Central Committee: Institutions, Measurement and Empirical Trends, 1978–2002," *CQ* 182 (2005): 338–355.

5. Andrew C. Mertha and Ka Zeng, "Political Institutions, Resistance and China's Harmonization with International Law," *CQ* 182 (2005): 309–337.

6. Elizabeth J. Remick, *Building Local States: China During the Republican and Post-Mao Era* (Cambridge, Mass.: Harvard University Asia Center, 2005).

7. Susan Shirk, *China, Fragile Superpower* (New York: Oxford University Press, 2007), 44, 175.

8. *People's Daily*, May 25, 2005.

9. Minxin Pei, *China's Trapped Transition: The Limits of Developmental Autocracy* (Cambridge, Mass.: Harvard University Press, 2006), 91.

10. WSJ, October 15, 2007; Frédéric Bobin, *Good Bye Mao?* (Paris: La Martinière, 2006), 159.

11. John P. Burns, " 'Downsizing' the Chinese State: Government Retrenchment in the 1990s," *CQ* 175 (2003): 775–802. Analogous projects have just been assigned to Li Keqiang: see SCMP, January 14, 2008.

12. AFP, Beijing, July 2, 2007.

13. SCMP, December 13, 2006.

14. Thierry Wolton, *Le grand bluff chinois* (Paris: Laffont, 2007), 40ff.

15. Andrew Wedeman, "The Intensification of Corruption in China," *CQ* 180 (2004): 895–921.

16. Bobin, *Good Bye Mao?*, 146; NW, October 3, 2005.

17. Willy Wo-Lap Lam, *Chinese Politics in the Hu Jintao Era* (Armonk, N.Y.: M. E. Sharpe, 2006), 215.

18. On the Sixteenth Congress, see the article by Joseph Fewsmith, "The Sixteenth National Party Congress: The Succession That Didn't Happen," *CQ*

173 (2003): 1–16; and Lowell Dittmer, "Leadership Change and Chinese Political Development," *CQ* 176 (2003): 903–925.

19. Wo-Lap Lam, *Chinese Politics in the Hu Jintao Era*, 18.

20. This point was well analyzed in SCMP, September 24 and October 12, 2007.

21. Shirk, *China, Fragile Superpower*, 72ff.

22. See the report by Valérie Niquet on the Seventeenth Congress of the CCP published on the Web site of the Institut français des Relations internationales.

23. Jean-Pierre Cabestan, "La montée en puissance de la diplomatie chinoise," in *Asie, dix ans après la crise*, ed. Sophie Boisseau du Rocher (Paris: La Documentation française, 2007), 71ff.; L, April 23, 2007.

24. IHT, June 23–24, 2007.

25. FT, August 1, 2007.

26. IHT, June 23–24, 2007.

27. SCMP, October 22, 2007; WSJ, October 22, 2007.

28. *China Today*, January 18, 2008; SCMP, November 22, 2007.

7. One People?

1. IHT, April 27, 2007; L, June 15, 2007.

2. David S. G. Goodman, "The Campaign to 'Open Up the West': National, Provincial-Level, and Local Perspectives," *CQ* 178 (2004): 317–334.

3. Susan Shirk, *China, Fragile Superpower* (New York: Oxford University Press, 2007).

4. Jean-Pierre Cabestan, "Les multiples facettes du nationalisme chinois," *Perspectives chinoises* 88 (2005): 28–42.

5. AFP, Beijing, July 9, 2007.

6. IHT, September 22, 2006.

8. Will China Finally Discover the World?

1. Gilbert Étienne, *Chine-Inde, le match du siècle* (Paris: Presses de Sciences Po, 1998).

2. LM, November 23, 2007.

3. There are interesting analyses of this offensive in the article by Jean Coussy and Jean-Jacques Gabbas published in *Alternatives internationales* (November 2007) as well as in the article by Philippe Richer in *Esprit* (October 2007).

4. Particularly that of Jean-Marc and Ydir Plantade, *La face cachée de la Chine* (Paris: Bourrin, 2006).

5. FT, September 6, 2006.
6. WSJ, September 3, 2007; AFP, Beijing, November 16, 2007. In addition, the head of the British secret services had to publicly warn the business world; see AFP, Beijing, December 1, 2007. Cases of Chinese espionage in Russia have also been noted. See also, for an example of spying on Russian ballistic technology, WSJ, December 3, 2007.
7. Marie-Claire Bergère, *Capitalisme et capitalistes en Chine* (Paris: Perrin, 2007).
8. LM, November 29, 2007; WSJ, December 12, 2007; IHT, February 20 and November 27, 2007.
9. LM, September 29, 2007; FT, April 12, 2007.
10. Chien-peng Chung, "The Shanghai Cooperation Organization: China's Changing Influence in Central Asia," *CQ* 180 (2004): 989–1009.
11. LM, January 17, 2007.
12. LM, December 22, 2007.
13. For the last year, a twofold blockage has appeared in the North Korean theater: in the first place, Pyongyang has again rejected international inspection of its nuclear installations, and for another, Kim Jong Il temporarily disappeared from view, apparently following a serious health crisis. As of January 2009, the issue is still open.
14. Peter Hays Grier, "China's 'New Thinking' on Japan," *CQ* 184 (2005): 831–850.

Conclusion: China's Great Challenge

1. See Jean-Luc Domenach, "Chine: Les balbutiements de l'histoire," *Critique internationale* 24 (2004): 81–103.
2. Benoît Vermander, *Chine brune ou Chine verte?* (Paris: Presses de Sciences Po, 2007), 79ff.
3. IHT, February 1, 2008.

Afterword: China Moves Toward a Consumer Economy

1. LM, February 29 and May 28, 2009; SCMP, March 2, 2009; NW, June 29, 2009; NYT, October 23, 2009; LC, July 4, 2011; Erik Izraëlewicz, *L'arrogance chinoise* (Paris: Grasset, 2011), 39.
2. "China Needs to Stimulate Reform, Not Only the Economy," FT, August 26, 2009; "China Needs Slower, Better Growth," FT, August 6, 2010. See also *Caijing* [Finance magazine], March 6, 2009; SCMP, March 6, 2009; FT, December 18, 2009.

3. LM, July 14 and 17, 2011; FT, January 21, 2011.

4. Izraëlewicz, *L'arrogance chinoise*, 17, 142.

5. NW, July 4, 2011; ALC, October 1, 2010.

6. TE, June 4, 2011; LM, June 22, 2010.

7. FT, May 16, 2011; LM, February 22, 2011.

8. FT, June 26–27, 2010; FT, February 16, 2011.

9. IHT, March 1, 2010; IHT, November 30, 2010.

10. For the spectacular example of the Taiwanese company Foxconn, see LM, August 3, 2011.

11. LM, January 23–24, 2011.

12. *Beijing Review*, September 8, 2011, 2.

13. See especially the assessment presented by Jean-Louis Rocca, *Une sociologie de la Chine* (Paris: La Découverte, 2010), 48–50; FT, February 9, 2009; *Beijing Review* June 2, 2011, 6; July 7, 2011, 2.

14. Izraëlewicz, *L'arrogance chinoise*, 182; AFP, January 1 and 14, 2010.

15. Izraëlewicz, *L'arrogance chinoise*, 199.

16. IHT, May 4–5, 2009; NW, August 31, 2010.

17. ALC, June 24, December 15, 2010.

18. IHT, November 12, 2010.

19. LM, October 23–24, 2011.

20. AFP, November 27, 2009. See also L, August 7, 2009; AFP, April 3, 2009; *Global Times*, November 26, 2009.

21. See, for example, the statements by Wen Jiabao during a trip to Guangdong, IHT, June 16, 2010.

22. Jean-Luc Domenach, "Chine: le successeur et la succession," *Politique internationale* 131 (Spring 2011).

Bibliography

Affeltranger, Bastien. "Haut voltage, haute voltige: Les ONG chinoises face aux barrages du Yunnan." *Monde chinois* 2, no. 1 (Winter 2005).

Agulhon, Maurice. *The Republic in the Village: The People of the Var from the French Revolution to the Second Republic.* Trans. Janet Lloyd. Cambridge: Cambridge University Press, 1982.

Attané, Isabelle. *Une Chine sans femmes.* Paris: Perrin, 2004.

Bergère, Marie-Claire. *Capitalisme et capitalistes en Chine.* Paris: Perrin, 2007.

Bianco, Lucien. *Les origines de la révolution chinoise, 1915–1945.* Paris: Gallimard, 2007.

Bobin, Frédéric. *Good Bye Mao?* Paris: La Martinière, 2006.

Bulard, Martine. *Chine-Inde, la course du dragon et de l'éléphant.* Paris: Fayard, 2008.

Burns, John P. "'Downsizing' the Chinese State: Government Retrenchment in the 1990s." *CQ* 175 (2003): 775–802.

Cabestan, Jean-Pierre, "La montée en puissance de la diplomatie chinoise." In *Asie, dix ans après la crise,* ed. Sophie Boisseau du Rocher, 57–80. Paris: La Documentation française, 2007.

———. "Les multiples facettes du nationalisme chinois." *Perspectives chinoises* 88 (2005): 28–42.

Cambreleng, Boris. *Faut-il avoir peur de la Chine?* Toulouse: Milan, 2006.

Cai, Yongshun. "Collective Ownership or Cadres Ownership? The Non-Agricultural Us of Farmland in China." *CQ* 175 (2003): 662–680.

Cheng Yingxiang and Claude Cadart. *Dégel de l'intelligence en Chine, 1976–1989.* Paris: Gallimard, 2004.

Choukroune, Leila. *La Chine et le maintien de la paix et de la sécurité internationale.* Paris: L'Harmattan, 1999.

Chung, Chien-peng. "The Shanghai Cooperation Organization: China's Changing Influence in Central Asia." *CQ* 180 (2004): 989–1009.

Cohen, Philippe, and Luc Richard. *La Chine sera-t-elle notre cauchemar?* Paris: Mille et une nuits, 2005.

Delmas-Marty, Mireille, and Pierre-Étienne Will, eds. *La Chine et la démocratie.* Paris: Fayard, 2007.

Dittmer, Lowell. "Leadership Change and Chinese Political Development." *CQ* 176 (2003): 903–925.

Domenach, Jean-Luc. *Aux origines du Grand Bond en avant, le cas d'une province chinoise.* Paris: Presses de la FNSP, 1982.

———. *Chine, l'archipel oublié.* Paris: Fayard, 1992.

———. "Chine: Le successeur et la succession." *Politique internationale* 131 (Spring 2011).

———. "Chine: Les balbutiements de l'histoire." *Critique internationale* 24 (2004): 81–103.

———. *Où va la Chine?* Paris: Fayard, 2002.

———. "Pékin pas si loin de Moscou!" In *Entre Kant et Kosovo,* ed. Anne-Marie Le Gloannec and Aleksander Smolar, 285–294. Paris: Presses de Sciences Po, 2003.

Edi, Maria. "State Capacity and Local Agent Control in China: CCP Cadre Management from a Township Perspective." *CQ* 173 (2003): 35–52.

Étienne, Gilbert. *Chine-Inde, le match du siècle.* Paris: Presses de Sciences Po, 1998.

———. *Chine-Inde, la grande compétition.* Paris: Dunod, 2007.

Faligot, Roger. *Les services secrets chinois de Mao aux JO.* Paris: Nouveau Monde, 2008.

Fewsmith, Joseph. "The Sixteenth National Party Congress: The Succession That Didn't Happen." *CQ* 173 (2003): 1–16.

Gipouloux, François. *La Chine du XXIe siècle: Une nouvelle super-puissance?* Paris: Armand Colin, 2006.

——. "La dynamique de l'économie chinoise et ses contraintes." In *Asie, dix ans après la crise,* , ed. Sophie Boisseau du Rocher, 19–44. Paris: La Documentation française, 2007.

Goodman, David S. G. "The Campaign to 'Open Up the West': National, Provincial-Level, and Local Perspectives." *CQ* 178 (2004): 317–334.

——. "Structuring Local Identity: Nation, Province, and County in Shanxi During the 1990s." *CQ* 172 (2002): 837–862.

Grier, Peter Hays. "China's 'New Thinking' on Japan." *CQ* 184 (2005): 831–850.

Guiheux, Gilles. "Le nouveau retournement des corps et des esprits en Chine, la mise à leur compte des travailleurs licenciés du secteur d'état." *L'Homme et la Société* 152–153 (2004): 97–127.

——. "Les nouvelles classes sociales chinoises: Comment penser les inégalités?" In *Asie, entre pragmatisme et attentisme,* ed. Sophie Boisseau du Rocher and François Godement, 17–32. Paris: La Documentation française, 2006.

Haski, Pierre. *Internet et la Chine.* Paris: Seuil, 2008.

——. *Le journal de Ma Yan.* Paris: Ramsay, 2002.

——. *Le sang de la Chine.* Paris: Grasset, 2005.

Hermet, Guy. *L'hiver de la démocratie.* Paris: Armand Colin, 2007.

Hochraich, Diana. *Pourquoi l'Inde et la Chine ne domineront pas le monde de demain.* Paris: Ellipses, 2007.

Holzman, Marie, and Bernard Debord. *Wei Jingsheng, un chinois inflexible.* Paris: Bleu de Chine, 2007.

Huang Yasheng. *Selling China: Foreign Direct Investments During the Reform Era.* Cambridge: Cambridge University Press, 2003.

Huo Dating. *La Chine sur le divan.* Paris: Plon, 2008.

Izraëlewicz, Erik. *L'arrogance chinoise.* Paris: Grasset, 2011.

——. *Quand la Chine change le monde.* Paris: Grasset, 2005.

Koller, Frédéric. *Portraits de Chine.* Paris: Alvik, 2004.

Lam, Willy Wo-Lap. *Chinese Politics in the Hu Jintao Era.* Armonk, N.Y.: M. E. Sharpe, 2006.

Lustgarden, Abraham. *China's Great Train.* New York: Times Books, 2008.

Mackerras, Colin. *China's Ethnic Minorities and Globalization.* London: Routledge-Curzon, 2003.

Massonnet, Philippe. *Pour en finir avec le miracle chinois.* Arles: Philippe Picquier, 2003.

Merle, Aurore, and Michael Sztanke. *Étudiants chinois: Qui sont les élites de demain?* Paris: Autrement, 2006.

Mertha, Andrew C. "China's 'Soft' Centralization: Shifting Tiao/Kuai Authority Relations." *CQ* 184 (2005): 791–810.

Mertha, Andrew C., and Ka Zeng. "Political Institutions, Resistance, and China's Harmonization with International Law." *CQ* 182 (2005): 309–337.

Naughton, Barry. *The Chinese Economy: Transitions and Growth.* Cambridge, Mass.: The MIT Press, 2006.

Naughton, Barry, and Dali L. Yang, eds. *Holding China Together: Diversity and National Integration in the Post-Deng Era.* Cambridge: Cambridge University Press, 2004.

Niquet, Valérie. *Chine-Japon: L'affrontement.* Paris: Perrin, 2006.

O'Brien, Kevin, and Li Lianjiang. *Rightful Resistance in Rural China.* Cambridge: Cambridge University Press, 2006.

Pairault, Thierry. "Formation initiale et développement économique." *Perspectives chinoises* 65 (2001): 5–16.

Pei, Minxin. *China's Trapped Transition: The Limits of Developmental Autocracy.* Cambridge, Mass.: Harvard University Press, 2006.

Plantade, Jean-Marc, and Ydir Plantade. *La face cachée de la Chine.* Paris: Bourrin, 2006.

Pun Ngai. *Made in China: Women Factory Workers in a Global Workplace.* Durham, N.C.: Duke University Press, 2005.

Remick, Elizabeth J. *Building Local States: China During the Republican and Post-Mao Era.* Cambridge, Mass.: Harvard University Asia Center, 2005.

Richer, Philippe. *La longue marche de la Chine en Afrique, 1504–2008.* Paris: Karthala, 2008.

Rocca, Jean-Louis. *La condition chinoise.* Paris: Karthala, 2006.

——. *Une sociologie de la Chine.* Paris: La Découverte, 2010.

Rowe, William T. *Crimson Rain: Seven Centuries of Violence in a Chinese County.* Palo Alto, Calif.: Stanford University Press, 2006.

Sheng, Yunmin. "Central-Provincial Relations at the CCP Central Committee: Institutions, Measurement and Empirical Trends, 1978–2002." *CQ* 182 (2005): 338–355.

Shirk, Susan. *China, Fragile Superpower.* New York: Oxford University Press, 2007.

Sorman, Guy. *The Empire of Lies: The Truth About China in the Early Twenty-First Century.* Trans. Asha Puri. New York: Encounter Books, 2008.

Tong, Yanqi. "Bureaucracy Meets the Environment: Elite Perceptions in Six Chinese Cities." *CQ* 189 (March 2007): 100–121.

Tsui, Kai-yuan, and Youqing Wang. "Between Separate Stoves and a Single Menu: Fiscal Decentralization in China." *CQ* 177 (2004): 71–90.

Vermander, Benoît. *Chine brune ou Chine verte?* Paris: Presses de Sciences Po, 2007.

Wedeman, Andrew. "The Intensification of Corruption in China." *CQ* 180 (2004): 895–921.

Wolton, Thierry. *Le grand bluff chinois*. Paris: Laffont, 2007.

Yang, Guobin. "Environmental NGOs and Institutional Dynamics in China." *CQ* 181 (2005): 46–66.

Index

biases, 121–22

billionaires, 19, 152

birth control policy, 53

blogs, 9

Bobin, Frédéric, 22

Bonapartism, 83

books, 7

Bo Xilai, 102, 154

Bo Yibo, 102

Brown, Gordon, 128

bureaucracy: elite, 98–100; independent, 113

campaign for education in patriotism, 116

Capgemini, 50, 78

capitalism, 17, 29, 120, 126–27; globalized, 23, 68

carbon dioxide emissions, 40

Carnegie Endowment, 168n16

CCP. *See* Chinese Communist Party

censorship, 7

center group, 153

Central Committee, of CCP, 20, 29, 95, 102, 105–6, 108, 153

central government, 8, 11, 14, 72, 85

Central Military Commission, 59, 106, 108

Central Party School, 105

Chen Yuan, 101

Chen Yun, 101, 103

Chevrier, Yves, 56, 167n60

Chiang Kai-shek, 87, 133

China Youth Daily, 10

Chinese Communist Party (CCP), 3–5, 38, 55, 99–100, 119, 152; Central Committee of, 20, 29, 95, 102, 105–6, 108, 153; Central Military

Commission of, 59; domination of, 155; internal cohesion of, 83; mistrust of, 137–38; Organization Department of, 13; Sixteenth Congress of, 105; Seventeenth Congress of, 9, 102, 104, 107, 136

Chinese medicine, 54

Chinese model, 171n13

Chinese moment, 47, 103, 114, 138

Chinese National Assembly and Senate, 76

Chinese People's Consultative Conference, 14

Chirac, Jacques, x

Christians, 121

cinema, control of, 7

citizenship, 36, 114, 115

civilized neighborhoods, 51

civil servants, 96, 97

class: consciousness, 21; enemies, 4; origins, 112; plutobureaucratic, 21–23, 106; struggle, 18–21; upper, 22

classification, 111, 121

climate change, 40

coal, 48; mines, 6, 39

commercial law, 23

communism: aristocracy and, 19; classification and, 111; discontent and, 73; disfavor of, 87; fall of, 24; history of, 24; rebellion against, 74; social democracy and, 61; totalitarian, 3; work units and, 11. *See also* Chinese Communist Party

Communist Youth League, 60, 105

companies: competition between, 16; foreign, 60, 63

conflicts: of distribution, 17; social, 18

espionage, 125
ethnic minorities, 92
European Commissioner for Consumer
  Protection, 124
European Union, 30, 128, 146
executions, 5. *See also* death penalty
exile, 111
exports, 34, 36, 124, 148; growth of, 95;
  scandals, 76
external world, 119, 120
extremes, proclivity for, 80–82

factional groupings, 85
factionalism, 104
factories, 38, 49
failure, 67–69
Falun Gong, 4, 98
families, aristocratic, 100–101
famine, 18
Far East, xi, 35
fiefdoms, 93
financial crisis: of 1997–1998, 65, 103;
  of 2008, 145–46
Financial Times, 146
folklore, 110
foreign companies, 60, 63
foreigners, 60
foreign imports, 41
foreign investors, 61, 77, 84
Foreign Ministry, 96, 126
foreign policy, 1, 26, 93, 97, 116
foreign presence, 158–59
foreign trade, ix, 27, 38, 149, 153
four modernizations, 56, 141
fragmentation: geography and, 11;
  territorial, 13
fragmented authoritarianism, 11

freedom, 15; individual, 28
French Economic Mission, 65

Gabbas, Jean-Jacques, 173n3
Gallic villages, 157
gas, 79
Geng Huichang, 125
geography: fragmentation and, 11;
  inequality and, 113
geopolitical disorder, 86
Gini coefficient, 18
Gipouloux, François, 41, 66
globalization, 27–29, 65, 129, 141;
  capitalism and, 23, 68
global status, 30–31
Gorbachev, Mikhail, 75
governance, 28
government: acid test for, 71–73; central,
  8, 11, 14, 72, 85; municipal, 9, 59
Great Leap Forward, 18
green economy, 146
growth, 34, 147; changes and, 35–37;
  control over, 56–58; decline in, 74; of
  exports, 95; human factors of, 47; rate,
  ix, 33, 65–67, 71; waste and, 38–41
guangxi (relations), 41
Guiheux, Gilles, 19
Guomindang, 144

Haber, Daniel, 66
harmonious society, 23, 56, 96, 135–38,
  142, 144
health care, 53–54, 150; reform of, 54–56
Hermet, Guy, 144
hierarchy, 121
high-end market, 61–62
Hochraich, Diana, 65

holy alliance, 77
hospitals, 53–54
Hu Deping, 103
Hu Haifeng, 101
Hu Jia, 83
Hu Jintao, 57–60, 84, 101–5, 123,
  136, 142, 153; corruption and, 97;
  harmonious society and, 23; military
  and, 107; succession and, 99
human development index, 37
human factors, of growth, 47
human rights, 1, 31, 76–77
hundred surnames, 16
hutongs, 47, 98
Hu Yaobang, 103
hypercitizens, 115

ideological revisions, 119
image, 36
IMF. *See* International Monetary Fund
imperialism, 116
imports, 34, 124; agricultural, 20;
  American, 139; foreign, 41
inadequacy, of state, 113–15
income: annual, 19; minimum payment,
  52; national, 106
India, 30, 49, 78, 91, 122–23
indiscipline, 80–82
individuality, 15
industrial counterfeiting, 61
industrial development, 39
industrialization, 20
industrial pollution, 40
industrial sectors, 38, 42
inegalitarianism, 113
inequality, 19, 83, 111–13, 151–54
inflation, 42, 139, 146

influence, of provincial leaders, 12
inheritances, 111
innovations, 6
institutionalization without
  democracy, 105
integration, 27, 41
intelligence apparatus, 27
intercultural dialogue, 29
internal democracy, 105
international aid, 37
International Development
  Association, 28
International Monetary Fund (IMF),
  122
Internet, control of, 8–9
investors, 49, 61, 77, 78, 84
iron rice bowl, 73
Izraëlewicz, Erik, 62

Japan, 30–31, 62, 116, 121, 132
jealousy, 151–54
Jiang Zemin, 26, 57–59, 84, 103, 107,
  113, 153
Jian Qing, 102
Jia Qinglin, 152
journalists, 82
June 1989 massacre, xi, 4, 107, 116
justice administration, 96

Kim Jong Il, 131, 174n13
Koizumi, Junichiro, 132

labor: contracts, 142; costs, 48–50;
  laws, 48. *See also* workers
language, 92
Lao Zhaopian (Old Photographs)
  (journal), 165n15

law, 4; bankruptcy, 42; commercial, 23; labor, 48
leaders, 75; betrayal by, 118; provincial, 12; Western, x. *See also specific leaders*
Lemoine, Françoise, 66
Levitte, Jean-David, x
liberalism, 23, 84
libraries, 60
Li Keqiang, 58, 99, 102, 104, 153
linguistics, 92; inheritances, 111
Li Peng, 101
Liu Shaoqi, 154
living standards, 38, 135
localisms, 94
local officials, 17–18
local predatory states, 12

mafias, 7, 69, 98, 130
managers, 61
mandarin, 126–27
Maoists, xi, 55–56, 67, 99; innovations of, 6; post-Maoism, 23–24; totalitarianism and, 3–6
Mao Zedong, 6, 24, 75, 116, 132, 140–42, 153; living conditions and, 71; mobilizations and, 14, 81; rebellion and, 18
markets: high-end, 61–62; Western, 76; world, 34. *See also* stock exchange system
marriage, 5
Marxism, 24
massacres: of June 1989, xi, 4, 107, 116; of Nanjing, 133
mass campaigns, 5, 81
media, 120; control of, 7–8; environmentalism and, 40

medicine, 54. *See also* health care
men, 5
mercantile policies, 28
merchants, 124; naïveté of, 126–27
Merkel, Angela, 123, 128
microclimates, 11–14
middle stratum, 19
migrant workers, 6, 49, 82
military, 106–8
militarism, 133
millionaires, 19, 151–52
minerals, 43
minimum income payment, 52
minimum wages, 50
mining, 6
Ministry of Justice, 96
Minxin Pei, 4, 12, 168n16
misperceptions, 37
mistrust, of Communist Party, 137–38
mobile phones, 8
mobilization, 81, 95, 109; spontaneous, 9; violent, 14
modernity, 55–56, 141–42
modernization: of economy, 34; four, 56, 141; of military, 106
money, 151. *See also* wealth
moral censure, 72
moralism, 158
Mugabe, Robert, 79
municipal government, 9, 59
Muslims, 92–93
mutual-assistance groups, 111

naïveté, 124, 126–27
naked development sites, 51
Nanjing massacre, 133
national income, 106

nationalism, 10, 60, 115–18, 120, 134

nationalization, 7

natural disasters, 11

natural resources, 48

navy, 106

neoconservatism, 19

neuroses, 131, 132

news media, control of, 7–8

newspaper cartoonists, 100

NGOs, 13–14, 87

Niquet, Valérie, 165n21

nonintervention in the affairs of states, 123

non-native zones, 92

official policy, 50

official propaganda, 11

oil, 43, 48, 79

Oksenberg, Michel, 11

Old Photographs (journal), 165n15

Olympic Games, 26, 36, 83–84, 117, 136, 145

opening, of China, 25–26, 27, 30

opinions: right to express, 15; Western, 77. *See also* public opinion

Opium Wars, 27, 56, 159

opportunism, 75

opposition activities, 7

optimism, 65, 69, 147

Organization Department, of CCP, 13

overpopulation, 152

overseas China, 110–11

Pan Yue, 40

party cells, 13

passports, 5

patriotism, 27, 99, 116

peacekeeping forces, 28

peasants, 12, 20–21, 51, 74, 115, 152

pedagogy, 63

People's Republic of China, 104, 121, 133

Permanent Committee of the Politburo, 159

pessimism, xi, 65

Peyrefitte, Alain, 80

pigeons, 76–80

pluralism, 143

plutobureaucratic class, 21–23, 106

police, 72; protection from, 13; raids, 81

policy, 68, 102; American, 30; anti-Soviet, 30; birth control, 53; economic, xii, 12; foreign, 1, 26, 93, 97, 116; of Japan, 31; mercantile, 28; official, 50; public, 114; recovery, 44; social, 51, 52, 94, 153; of trade, 31

Politburo, 58, 95, 99, 102, 105–6; Permanent Committee of, 159

politics, return of, 82–85

political liberalism, 84

political prisoners, 4

political system, 93

politicization, 14; of rural communities, 13

pollution, 39, 59; of air, 40; coal and, 48; industrial, 40

popular unrest, 82

population, 37, 53, 91; confidence of, 140; division of, 115; overpopulation, 152; plutobureaucracy and, 22

populism, 134

post-Maoism, 23–24

poverty, 38, 110

power, xi; arbitrary, 36; centralized, 95; increasing, 135; soft, 65

social classes. *See* class
social conflict, 18
social difference, 51
social emancipation, 17
social envelopment, 22
social happiness, 159
socialism, 61, 74
social modernity, 56
social overlapping, 72
social policy, 51, 52, 94, 153
social welfare payments, 52
society of small prosperity, 135
soft power, 65
solitude, 150
Songhua River, 59
sons of princes, 101–2, 153–54
Sorman, Guy, 12, 64
Southern Weekend (publication), 8
Soviet Union, 30, 41, 74, 87
spatial equalization, 113
special interest mafias, 69
specialized administrations, 96
spontaneous mobilization, 9
stability, 98
stabilization, 30
Stalin, Joseph, 24
Standard and Poor, 66
standard Chinese, 92
Standing Committee, 105, 106
state: inadequacy of, 113–15; local
    predatory, 12; nonintervention in the
    affairs of, 123; officials, 96
State Council Information Office, 8
State Environmental Protection
    Administration, 40
stock exchange system, 42–43, 79–80
strategic weapons, 106

Strauss-Kahn, Dominique, 122
subcitizens, 115
subversion, 83
suffering, 73–74
suicide, 5
Sun Yat-sen, 87, 109
supertrain, 10
Supreme Court, 5, 96
surveillance, 5
suspicions, 118

tactical weapons, 106
Taiwan, 94, 107, 131, 133–34, 143
taxes: agricultural, 20; proliferation
    of, 94
technology, 59, 127; espionage, 125
territory: control over, 113;
    fragmentation of, 13
terrorism, 131
Third World countries, 64
Three Gorges Dam, 40
Tiananmen Square, 4
Tianjin earthquake, 37
Tibetans, 92, 93
Time of the Planet (magazine), 121
Tocqueville, Alexis de, 84
torture, 5
totalitarianism, 87; analogous
    movements and, 10; control methods
    of, 82; end of, 3–6; isolation and, 25
tourism, 28, 149, 155
trade, 123; connections, 59; foreign, ix,
    27, 38, 149, 153; legislation, 129;
    policy of, 31; surpluses, 34, 43. *See
    also* World Trade Organization
travelers, 16
trials, 4

UN. *See* United Nations

UNCTAD, 78

unions, 60

United Nations (UN), 26, 48

United States, 122, 128; anti-Americanism, 117; imports of, 139; policy, 30; returnees from, 117; Sino-American dialogue, 119

unity, 91–94

Universal Exposition, 66, 67, 145

university system, 62–64

upper class, 22

urbanization, 40, 150

urban renewal, 10

Vermander, Benoît, 163n6

very poor, 52

villages, 152; elections of, 13; Gallic, 157

violence, 29, 86, 144; mobilization and, 14

wages, 48–49; minimum, 50

wage costs, 50

Wahaha firm, 78, 116

Wal-Mart, 60, 82

waste, growth and, 38–41

water, 39

wealth, 19, 151–52

weapons, 106

Wei Jinsheng, 1

welfare, 52; public, 113, 114

Wen Jiabao, 10, 84, 101, 146, 153; harmonious society and, 23; social policies and, 51

West: attraction to, 26; employers of, 16; idealizing of, 117; leaders of, x;

liberalism of, 23; markets of, 76; opinions of, 77; overestimation of, 122; public opinion of, 124; research and, 63

Wolton, Thierry, 171n13

women, 5–6

workers: migrant, 6, 49, 82; mobility of, 16

workshop industries, 78

work units, 11, 52, 73

World Bank, 28, 66

world hierarchy, x

world market, 34

world society, 124

world standards, 37

World Trade Organization (WTO), 26, 56, 65, 95, 129

World War II, 132

written language, 92

WTO. *See* World Trade Organization

xenophobia, 27, 28

xiagang ("those who stepped down from their posts"), 52

Xi Jinping, 58, 99, 102, 104, 153–54

Xi Zhongxun, 102

Yasukuni Jinja, 132

Yu Keping, 29

Yu Yaobang, 102

Yu Yongding, 146

Zeng Qinghong, 102, 103–4, 123

Zhao Ziyang, 102

Zhou Enlai, 14, 101

Zhu Rongji, 26, 68, 72

Zong Qinghou, 116

951.06   Domenach, Jean-Luc.
DOM
              China's uncertain
              future.

                                  8-13

$32.50

DATE			